Maxine Harper's
Journey of Hope

A Memoir

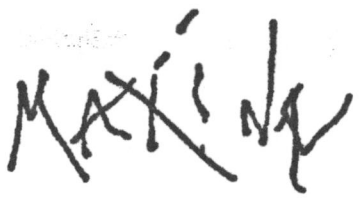

Post Office Box 1658 • Greenwood, Mississippi 38935-1658

Maxine Harper's Journey of Hope
© 2009 by Maxine Harper

Printed and bound in the United States of America. All rights reserved. No part of this publication may be reproduced in any form or by any electronic or mechanical means, including information storage and retrieval systems, without permission in writing from the publisher, except in the case of brief passages quoted in a printed review.

Published by Lantern Publishing Company.
Post Office Box 1658, Greenwood, Mississippi 38935-1658
First Edition. First Printing 2009.

"Welcome to Holland" was written by Emily Perl Kingsley,
© 1987 by Emily Perl Kingsley. All rights reserved.
Reprinted by permission of the author.

Graphic design and layout by Wanda Harper Clark.

ISBN 978-0-9653097-2-1

Library of Congress Control Number: 2009901681

Acknowledgments

In this section of the book, the author typically pays recognition to those persons who had a special role in the book's origin and/or completion. Although this book began as my memoirs, it has evolved into something infinitely greater. More than simply describing the notable events in my life, this book describes many of the people who helped to make possible the rich and rewarding life I have enjoyed in the midst of seemingly overwhelming physical odds. In this respect, this is a book of acknowledgments.

Some of the people whom you will meet in the coming pages deserve special recognition for the direct role they played in this book's production. As with all my ventures, my parents, Max and Bernice Harper, have been my stalwart supporters without whom the many successes in my life would not have been possible. To them I owe my unending gratitude.

In addition to the love and support she has given me as her sister, I am also grateful to Wanda Harper Clark for contributing her graphic talents to the design and layout of this book.

My niece, Avent Clark, has brought me a special love, joy, and wisdom that reflect her own vibrant personality. Her presence in my life is a priceless gift.

With a few close friends and relatives, I shared the feeble beginnings of this book. My thanks go to Patsy, Emmy, Rosemary, and Betty for advising and encouraging me as I began the journey of writing my memoirs.

As God would have it, though, it was through Allyn, an acquaintance who became an intimate friend, that this book made its way to completion. Allyn read my chapters a few at a time and met with me on a regular basis to share her enthusiasm for my work. Her comments about my chapters were always the same – "I love them!" God must have known that I needed someone's frequent smile of approval, someone's tangible hug of encouragement, to complete the work He had laid out for me to do. And so He sent Allyn. And to Allyn I will be forever grateful for cheering me on to the finish line.

Finally, this book would not be complete without the finishing touches of Kathleen, whose friendship spans nearly three decades and whose oneness with my mind and heart is a rare and precious gift.

Prologue

I was three-fourths of the way through writing this book when I realized it had no message, or at least not the message I intended it to have. I almost ditched the book altogether. But I had promised it to too many people who honestly wanted to hear my story. I decided that if I could dig deep within my soul and find something of value to share with the rest of humanity, I would finish the book. If you see this prologue in print, you will know I succeeded.

In the first chapter I wrote about what cerebral palsy took away from me – in a word, physical freedom – the freedom to walk, feed and dress myself, and basically live independently. But this is not what this book is about. This book is about what God has given me in return – a faith to believe that He is able to take something that could be considered devastating and turn it into something that can glorify Him.

He has given me a family whose love and devotion cannot be matched. He has given me friends who have eyes that do not look away from my broken shell but look beneath it to build up the spirit within.

God has allowed me to travel to lands that are foreign to most people. I've been to the land of inhumanity, only to escape into arms of dignity and love. I've traveled the road of helplessness and fear, only to find guardian angels by my side. I've entered the land of the most excruciating pain, only to get a glimpse of the land where there will be no pain. I've journeyed into the valleys of hopelessness and despair, only to be permitted to climb the mountains of triumph and gladness.

God has shown me sights that few have ever seen. He has shown me the silent love of a child who cannot speak; He has shown me the hope of the daffodil; and He has let me see the first buds of compassion on faces too young to have known the roots of such emotion.

God has let me hear laughter in the midst of tears, music in the midst of turmoil, and the whisper of hope above the noise of discontent.

If you find sorrow in these pages, may you also find joy. If you find pain, may you also find the balm of healing. If you find a twinge of loneliness, may you also find the hugs of friendship. Most of all, through these pages, as you share my journey, may you feel the same One holding your hand who has held mine.

Life's Beginnings

The clock in the waiting room outside labor and delivery had the brand name Simplex written across its face. It stared at me, and I stared back. Somehow, the name struck me as a contradiction to the setting. Giving birth was no simple matter. Things could go wrong – horribly wrong.

As I sat there in my wheelchair waiting for my sister's baby to be born, thoughts of my own traumatic birth mingled strangely with the anticipation of the joy that lay ahead. This birth will be fine, I assured myself, praying desperately that it would be so. My sister Wanda, of course, knew that our mother had experienced great difficulty in giving birth to me, and Wanda had shared that background with her own obstetrician. I hoped he would take extra precautions.

Our phone had rung in the wee hours of the morning on August 7, 1987. My brother-in-law said, "You need to come on down so you'll be here when the baby comes." My mother, half asleep, mumbled, "What time is it anyway?" Oh, the ribbings she got from that!

It was around 4:30 a.m. when Daddy lifted me into the station wagon, tossed my chair in the back, and we began the two-hour drive to the hospital. Strangely, I remember so vividly the fog that traveled with us. I remember praying in brief spurts, praying that Wanda would have an easy delivery, praying that the baby would be all right. I wanted my prayers to be a long, concentrated communion with God; instead, I found my attention to be too broken by anxious thoughts. I hoped God would understand.

The sun was just coming up as we drove into the hospital parking lot. Wanda's friend Ann met us and told us that Wanda had not delivered yet. We took our place in the waiting room with friends and relatives who were also anxiously awaiting this birth. Time passed slowly. The baby, we were told, was in no danger; but after 12 hours of labor, he or she just wasn't making any progress down the birth canal. There were two choices – use long forceps or perform a C-section. Without question, Wanda chose the C-section. Relief spread through me. Now there would be less danger that the same thing would go wrong again.

So it was that at 10:35 that morning, my brother-in-law emerged, still dressed in his green scrubs, cradling in his arms the most beautiful and perfectly formed baby girl I had ever seen. Seven pounds, six ounces, with blue eyes that squinted in the light to which she was unaccustomed. Her Daddy said proudly, "This is Avent Meriwether Clark." Then he quipped, "I knew it was a girl. She was too stubborn to come out."

I had only a moment to gaze in wonder at my niece before she was whisked away to the nursery. We followed close behind – a small caravan that included my parents and the friends and relatives who had waited so eagerly to see this new little one, this "fresh baby," as she was called by her Daddy. The doctor, pulling off his surgical cap, met us in the hall. "Wanda gave it all she had," he said, "but she had gone long enough. We did a C-section, and everything's fine." His eyes met mine for a brief moment, and I could imagine him thinking, "Ah, yes, she's the reason Wanda wanted nothing to do with forceps."

We proceeded to the nursery, where we could gaze to our hearts' content at this new little life. The viewing window was high, so I alternated between sitting on pillows and standing supported by my parents. I watched as the nurse bathed and diapered the small red body whose legs kicked and lungs screamed out in protest. She was healthy and already filled with a zest for living.

As joy and relief spread through me, a strange sensation tugged at my heart. Looking at this tiny baby with her new life before her, I saw what might have been for me – and what would never be. Tears of joy mingled with tears of grief and made them inseparable.

Some 32 years earlier, I too had emerged from my mother's womb. But I had not been gently lifted out, as Avent was, and as I should have been. Instead, forceps gripped my head and forced my 8-pound, broad-shouldered body through an opening that was too small for it. Birth trauma, they call it. I entered the world quietly – no crying, indeed, no breathing. The doctor resuscitated me and placed me on a ventilator that had been donated to the hospital only two weeks earlier by a generous couple whose newborn had died for lack of such equipment. Now this special ventilator was used to draw precious air into my lungs.

With my life hanging in the balance, the doctor went to my father that night, not with the expected news of the joyous arrival of his firstborn, but rather with the painful message, "You have a little girl. But I must tell you she had a rough time getting here, and she may not make it through the night. Would you like to see her?"

Within moments the doctor was leading my father down the corridor to the nursery, a place that was usually off limits to everyone except hospital staff. I wonder what Daddy thought when he saw me for the first time. Could he tell that my eyes were shaped like his? Was he afraid he might never hold me? I've never asked him. I'm not sure I could bear the pain I would see on his face.

My parents had married late in life, at least compared with the norm of their day. Mama was 27 and Daddy 33 when Daddy's elder brother tied the knot on a hot day in June 1951 – a day so hot that the candles melted. Mama likes to say that Daddy's family had given up on his ever getting married. She also likes to brag that she was being "choosy" in waiting so long to marry. But that was only the beginning of their waiting. It was three years later before Mama finally became pregnant. Daddy was thrilled! The men in his family are known for adoring little babies.

Mama had an uneventful pregnancy, with her only recollection being her craving for Snickers and Coke. Her due date was September 2, 1955. Labor pains awakened her on the morning of September 1st and lasted throughout the day as she bided her time in the hospital. By 9 o'clock that night, the doctor was tired of waiting and ready to go home. "Let's go see if we can have that baby," he urged. This baby wasn't quite ready to be born, and a foiled delivery resulted.

Back in her hospital room, Mama drifted in and out of sleep, heavy with sedation and only faintly aware that her newborn was in distress. Daddy sat with her and waited. An hour passed, then two, three, four, five hours. Finally, around 2 a.m., the doctor appeared again, this time with the news, "I think she's going to make it."

Thus began my life. The struggle to survive now became a struggle to do more than just exist. It became a struggle to live.

After 17 days in the hospital, my mother was finally well enough for the two of us to go home. The deep gashes left in my head by the forceps were healing, and my round face and chubby legs made me look like a very ordinary baby. And since all infants have a wobbly head and uncoordinated movements, mine gave no cause for alarm. Thinking that I had passed through the crisis safely, my parents happily took me home.

I was named Lela Maxine – Lela after my mother (Lela Bernice), and Maxine after my father (Maxie Allen). They decided to call me Maxine. I had a smattering of light brown hair and blue eyes that later turned brown.

I appeared to be a healthy baby, except for severe bouts of colic. But as the weeks of my infancy passed, my parents grew puzzled. When they laid me down, I would always be in the same place when they came back. I didn't scoot over to one corner of the bed; I didn't even turn over. My head wasn't getting any steadier either, and my hands were fisted and not coordinated enough to hold anything. I even had trouble sucking milk from my bottle. Daddy recalls punching a hole in the nipple with an ice pick. When he told me about it later, I wondered how he knew what to do. He grinned and said, "Well, I had to do something to stop you from squalling."

Months went by; and though I was growing and smiling and noticing people, little else had changed. I wasn't even close to being able to crawl or even sit alone. The pediatrician finally admitted that he had been suspecting a problem for some time. Now it was impossible to ignore it. He explained that I had nerve damage. That was it – no name, no prognosis. Just wait and see.

By the time my niece Avent was born, I had lived 32 years with what turned out to be quadriplegic cerebral palsy, the result of damage to the part of my brain that controls my muscles. The time I spent deprived of oxygen during birth had left its ugly mark. Cerebral palsy is a thief; in its worst form, it robs its victims of the freedom most people take for granted – the freedom to use their limbs to do their bidding and to use their mouths to speak their thoughts effortlessly. By the time Avent was born, though, I had also lived long enough to outsmart the thief. Cerebral palsy did indeed rob my body, but it didn't touch my mind or my spirit. Despite early predictions that I would never go to school, I graduated as valedictorian of my high school class and went on to earn a doctorate degree and finally to teach in a university.

As I have traveled through life, I have learned to trust God as the Giver – the Giver who gives back twofold everything that is taken away. In place of a body that can never hope to achieve agility and fitness, He has given me a spirit that can run free. To replace uncoordinated hands, He has given me a mind that loves to finger the depths of knowledge. To compensate for speech that will never be fluent, He has placed in my path people who truly listen; and He has put His own pen in my mind and heart.

God has given me in abundance the love and devotion of family and friends. He has given me parents and a sister who have held nothing back in their determination to help me live a quality life. He has made my extended family of aunts, uncles, and cousins become more like my immediate family, with bonds beyond rival. He has given me friendships that are deep and abiding, devoid of frivolous pretense. People who would be fair weather friends run the other way, leaving only the truest of friends. With them, as with my family, there is a unique bond of love and trust. I can reveal my frailties unabashedly, knowing that I will be treated with gentleness and respect.

My sister Wanda, in addition to offering a lifetime of friendship and care, has given me something no one else could. From the time Avent was born, Wanda has allowed me to be a part of her life. I have experienced some of the joys of motherhood that I feared would never be mine. That realization came to me one day as I watched Avent running across the walkway from my parents' house to mine. A smile crept across my face. She ran freely, with all the joy of a young child unhampered by anything. "Thank God she can run," I thought! My intellect told me that she would have been born safely even if my own birth trauma had never come to light. But some part of me wanted to believe that through my life, I had made some minute contribution to her chance to live a life of freedom. In that split second, I realized that I, her Mackie, loved her so much that my own shackles felt a little lighter simply because she had none.

Perhaps this is the secret after all. It's easy to know what you've lost. The secret lies in appreciating what you've been given.

Tenderly Loved

The room was cold and unfamiliar. I was only three years old, and I hadn't been inside a hospital since I was born. Now nurses in white caps were standing around the table where I sat, supported by my mother's hands. As my mother began unbuttoning my shirt, she reassured me that they were just going to take a picture of my neck. But the big machine over the table frightened me, and I wailed as it was brought down very close to my body.

Of course, the X-rays revealed no problem with my neck that would cause my head to be so wobbly. Later it was obvious that the problem went much deeper than that. But the X-ray incident marked one of the first memories from my early childhood. It was my first signal that life would be different for me.

Except for a few isolated moments, however, my first four years of life blend together in my memory as one day that patterned itself after all the others. I remember the big old two-storied house where we lived. Downstairs there was a huge living room – large enough for me to ride my specially built tricycle in! A beautiful grand piano gave a sense of majesty and character to that room. The kitchen, old-fashioned in its appearance, allowed winter drafts to blow through it freely, often carrying the aroma of freshly baked biscuits. Rarely did I see the upstairs rooms, though I remember that the bathrooms were characterized by the exquisite marble of older days.

We moved into the "big house" when I was only two years old. By then, I had a younger sister, Wanda, born just ten days before my first birthday. My mother's parents – "Annie" and "Pappy" as we called them – had also come to live with us. And since I couldn't walk and my grandparents couldn't climb stairs very well, the six of us huddled into the two downstairs bedrooms.

Those were days of comfort and security for me. My family adapted day by day to my physical limitations. They bought a special over-sized baby walker that I could maneuver with my feet, thus giving me some mobility. I still had no sitting balance; so Pappy, who was a carpenter, built wooden sides onto our little red wagon, and Annie padded it with pillows and pulled Wanda and me around in it. Also, since I couldn't sit in a regular swing, Pappy built a box seat for me and hung it from our swing set. I loved to swing so high it felt like I was touching the trees.

When doctors and therapists recommended that I try to stand for a while each day, Pappy built a "standing box" that would hold me upright. There was a little door in the back of the box that opened into a small round cut-out where I stood. A tray extended in front of me, and there I could play with toys or try my

JULY 1962

hand at coloring while I practiced standing. Mama encouraged me to stand in the box as long as I could, but she always willingly unlatched the little door and lifted me out when my legs grew tired.

Days in the big house were happy and tranquil. Early in the mornings, when the blackberries were ripe, Annie would put me in the stroller and take me with her to pick berries from the vines along the alley behind our house. Sometimes, in the winter, we ate breakfast by the heater in the bedroom because the kitchen was so drafty. During the days, Annie read to Wanda and me by the hour as we sat on the swinging glider on the screened porch that wrapped around the house. Again and again, we begged to hear the story of "The Little Mailman on Mulberry Lane." Our play room was that porch, filled with toys, though the only one I remember distinctly was a rubber doll that I called "Blue Foot" because he had blue shoes painted on his feet.

Nighttime baths were a family affair. Daddy set me in the tub, where I leaned against Mama's tummy. Wanda sat at the other end. When we were finished bathing and playing in the water, Daddy came and lifted his little girls out one at a time, dried us off and dressed us in our pajamas. Then the four of us crawled into one bed, with Wanda and me in the middle. There we talked and laughed until it was time to go to our own beds. One night when we were all together, Wanda said, "Here we are – three women and a boy." I suppose Daddy was outnumbered, but I don't think he minded one little bit.

My world at that time was small and secure. Though my hands were fisted and my arms lacked enough coordination to allow me to feed myself, there were always other hands ready to feed a hungry child. I couldn't sit without support either, but there was always a soft and loving lap ready to hold me. And oh, how everyone rejoiced over the things I could do! I learned to spell my name at an early age, and the praise bestowed on me was no less than that heaped upon a Nobel Prize winner. I had begun talking at a normal age, though my speech was strained and not so easily understood by strangers. Still, my family understood me precisely. Those early years, bathed with such unconditional love and acceptance, bestowed on me a sense of my own identity and value that would remain with me forever.

A Different World

I sat in my mother's lap for the entire 100-mile trip to Jackson that January day in 1960. My family seldom went farther than to visit my father's family some 17 miles away in the country, and on those trips I usually sat in the car seat and Wanda in Mama's lap. But this trip was different. Wanda stayed at home with Annie and Pappy, and the car seemed strangely quiet as my parents and I rode along in silence. It seemed that Mama held me unusually close.

I knew I was going to school, but I didn't know I was going to live there. When we arrived at the long brick building with the words "Mississippi Hospital School for Cerebral Palsy" written across the front, Daddy carried me inside to a sterile-looking lobby. To the left there was a group of padded seats with alternating orange and yellow vinyl cushions. To the right there was a high counter-like desk, behind which a receptionist stood. Soon a uniformed worker appeared, bringing with her a large wooden wheelchair. Following instructions, Daddy set me in the chair. It was my first time ever to sit in a wheelchair. Bewildered, I then watched as luggage was brought in and left on the floor in the lobby. I surmised that it must be my luggage.

At the tender age of four, I found myself being hugged good-bye by my parents and left in surroundings that were cold and impersonal. Of course, I didn't understand that my parents were simply following the advice of "experts" who had convinced them that, with a little therapy, I could learn to walk, use my hands, and speak more clearly. I had no way of knowing that Mama and Daddy saw this as their one opportunity for giving me a more normal future. I knew only that this was a lonely and frightening place.

As the house mother wheeled me down a long corridor, anguished tears streamed down my face. There was no consoling hug from her, no comforting dialogue. She said only, "Be sure to tell me when you need to go to the bathroom."

When we reached the large open gathering room that was referred to as "the hall," I was still crying, overcome with confusion and fear. The house mother wheeled me over to an aquarium in a far corner of the room. "Here," she said, "watch the fish for a while." I didn't want to watch the fish. I wanted to go home. But it would be two weeks before I could see my parents again – this was my "adjustment period."

I don't remember how long I cried. In my heart I don't think I ever really stopped crying. In that one moment, I felt as though I had lost my identity as a child and had become a "thing" that required routine physical maintenance.

Even the director of the facility used me as an exhibit. When he escorted visitors through the building, he would come to me and ask me to stretch out my hand so they could see it shake; then he would introduce me as "our little athetoid" (in reference to the type of cerebral palsy I had) – no human name required. In fact, I remember looking around in the cafeteria one day and thinking, "I must not be human like these adults are; but if I'm not human, then what am I?"

Despite my sadness, I quickly learned the layout of this place where I would spend the next four years. There were five pairs of children's rooms encircling the hall, with a nurse's station at one end of the hall. Five beds lined three walls of each room. For each pair of rooms there was a bathtub room in the middle. The large window in each room was covered with heavy drapes that always remained closed. Each child had only a bed with rails and a small closet with a shelf. We could each have one toy. I remember taking with me a stuffed yellow dog named Snoopy to cuddle with.

There was a morning house mother from 6:00 a.m. until 2:00 p.m., then another from 2:00 p.m. until 10:00 p.m. Each house mother was charged with caring for the children in one pair of rooms (8 to 10 children) during her shift. But caring in this case usually meant caring only for our most basic physical needs, if that. One house mother was so cruel that I was afraid to ask her to take me to the bathrom; instead, I would wet my pants, delaying any interaction with her as long as possible. Sure, she scolded me even more for soiling my clothes, but in my young mind a scolding at a later time was more bearable than confronting her harshness at the moment.

For better or worse, we changed house mothers every three months. The rationale was that we should not become too attached to one person. So we constantly had to get used to someone new.

Everything in that place was done with a mechanical roteness. We were awakened each morning, not by a welcoming voice, but by the bright light being flicked on by the incoming house mother. One by one, we were dressed, not in clothes of our own choosing, but in whatever shirt and shorts happened to be on top of the stack on our shelf. We had to wear shorts year round to accommodate the metal braces on our legs.

Dressed for the day, we were wheeled to the cafeteria for breakfast. The nurse came around with a handful of plastic spoons and poured liquid vitamins into each tiny mouth. Breakfast usually consisted of a biscuit and eggs (sometimes dehydrated eggs) or a bowl of oatmeal. Children who had to be fed (and that included me) were seated one on each side of an adult feeder who moved the spoons rotely to our mouths. I don't remember ever being asked what I wanted a bite of next or even being talked to at all during the meal. I do remember being slapped on the hand for not chewing fast enough.

Lunch was conducted the same way as breakfast. We ate what was spooned into our mouths, and I have no recollection of anything tasting good. I remember only sameness – tapioca pudding, fruit cocktail, bland food. Only on Sundays did we have a meal such as roast beef, mashed potatoes, green peas, and rolls.

During the week, "classes" began at 8:30 and ended at 4:30. There was physical therapy twice a day, occupational therapy, speech therapy, "school," and sometimes (rarely) music or a play period. Although the therapists and teachers worked with us individually, few bonds were formed. It was as though we were mechanical devices gone awry, and the workers' job was to "fix" us. I remember hearing little praise, because most of us weren't "fixable" according to their definitions. I remember only being scolded for not trying.

In "school" the teacher handed me a basal reader and said, "When you come to a word you don't know, ask me." On other occasions she told me to practice my penmanship for the whole period. What a waste! My handwriting would never be legible. My only recollection of anything "fun" was when my teacher learned that I had a knack for spelling and she taught me to spell words like "antidisestablishmentarianism." I never knew what it meant, only that I received recognition and praise for spelling it for anyone whom my teacher wanted to impress. In those days I'd do anything for a word of praise.

Speech therapy was sort of strange. I don't remember learning any techniques that would improve my speech. I do recall having peanut butter smeared throughout my mouth and being told to rake it out with my tongue.

In occupational therapy I had metal-laden cuffs placed on my tiny arms in an effort to keep them from flailing about. It didn't help; it only made it more painful when my hand got away from me and I knocked myself in the face. There was one positive thing that came from occupational therapy, though. It was there that I learned to use a typewriter with a keyguard over the keys. The keyguard was a metal template with a hole for each key. I could strike the key I wanted without striking a host of other keys with my fist. "Typing" was fun, probably the only activity in which I felt some sense of success. I would write letters home – only a few simple sentences; nevertheless, I was doing something I considered productive.

Physical therapy was the hardest part of the day. My task was to learn to walk. Girded with braces on my legs and a helmet on my head, I was placed upright on my feet. The therapist, sitting on a rolling stool in front of me, commanded me to walk. The therapy room seemed to stretch forever as I made one tiny, struggling step after another. The pain of trying to walk increased with each step I took. My knees, bent by the contractures from the cerebral palsy, ached under the strain. I begged to sit down and rest. "If you can just make it to the mirror," said the therapist. But the full-length mirror she was referring to was halfway down the length of the room. Sometimes I made it to the mirror without falling; most times I didn't. Even when I did, I felt no sense of accomplishment, for I knew that this painful experience wasn't walking – and for me it never would be. Nevertheless, it would be repeated the next day.

"Classes" ended at 4:30. At no time during the day did we go outside to play or even just to feel the sunshine. The therapy rooms were located in the interior portion of the building where there were no windows. So basically we were shut off from the outside world.

At 5:00 we were taken to the cafeteria for the evening meal. The menu never varied during the entire four years I spent there. On Mondays, Wednesdays, and Fridays, we were served hash and biscuits. On Tuesdays, it was hot dogs; on Thursdays and Saturdays, hamburgers; and on Sundays, sandwiches.

Soon after the evening meal, bath time began. One by one, we were bathed, with no changing of the water between children. Our hair was washed once a week – on Friday nights – and left to dry overnight. After our baths, we were dressed in our pajamas and put into bed as quickly as possible, often while the sun was still high in the sky. It wasn't hard to figure out that our caretakers were ready to be done with us for the day.

During the night hours no house mothers were on duty. Only a nurse and an aide were there to monitor 40 children, and our calls for help typically went unheard.

There were no "classes" on Saturdays. That was the day I simply sat through, longing for Sunday, when my family could visit. There were many Saturday nights when sleep eluded me, so eager was I to be with my family again.

I could choose what I wanted to wear on Sundays, so I would lie awake and decide which dress was my favorite. I was also spared from wearing my braces on Sundays – a delightful reprieve. One Sunday after Mama had bought me a pair of black patent "Sparkle Toe" shoes, my house mother tried to dress me in an older pair of shoes, but I resisted, saying, "I don't want those shoes. I want my ten dollar shoes!"

When Sunday finally made its long-awaited appearance every week, I was one of the more fortunate children. My name was among the first to be called every Sunday afternoon at 1 o'clock. My parents were never late to pick me up;

and Annie, Pappy, and Wanda were always with them. We had only three hours together, and there was not a minute to lose.

We had relatives in the area, and often we spent our time together in their homes. On other Sundays, when the weather was pretty, we visited in the park. We ate, talked, hugged, and treasured our time together.

My joy at being with my family was clouded only by the realization that the clock was ticking, and all too soon I would have to return to that long brick building devoid of all the love and enjoyment that childhood is meant to have. I wept at each separation as though it was the first, and only in adulthood did I learn that my family also wept after leaving me each time.

So it was that as joyful as Sunday mornings were, Sunday evenings were equally as sad. The staff made no effort to ease the pain of separation. In fact, one house mother, seeing that I was on the verge of tears one Sunday night, threatened to put me in isolation if I wept. Fortunately, I was able to squelch the tears until she left the room. Then I buried my face in my pillow so no one would hear me crying.

As young as I was, though, I found comfort in my Bible – holding it in my hands and reading the words I recognized. I remember some of the loneliness melting away as I tried to read my Bible. Of course, I was too young to really comprehend what I was reading, but it felt like God was there with me.

Surely there were some enjoyable events during those four years – something pleasant in my book of memories. Yes, the Shriners took us to the state fair every fall. How I looked forward to that! I remember being so amazed at how kind they were to us. They gently set us on the rides and bought whatever we wanted to eat. Most astonishingly, they treated us as though we were special to them, as though they enjoyed being with us. Even the housemothers who went with us were kind to us then. Wonder why!

Although we weren't actually allowed to have visitors, one evening when I was in the cafeteria a worker came and told me I had a visitor. The other children watched with envy as I was wheeled away to the lobby. I couldn't imagine who would be visiting me. When I got to the lobby, there sat my Uncle Moss. He had come to Jackson for a meeting and had stopped in to see me. "How're you doing, punkin?" he asked as he gave me a hug. We talked for a few minutes before he had to leave, but those few minutes of being cared about by someone have stuck with me the rest of my life.

Surely there were also some good staff members at the long brick building. Yes, one house mother said prayers at night with each child in her care. One nurse let me have apple juice before bedtime. Once, a house mother even bought a gift for me to give my mother for her birthday. Another house mother let me listen to the radio at night. But there were others who threatened punishment for whimpering when a shot was administered, or for asking that pinching braces be loosened. The care and concern I longed for came only in isolated incidents; and for the most part, everything was cold and impersonal. I was young, and I missed being held, read to, and listened to, without being afraid.

In writing this chapter, I remember the vow I made to be grateful for what I've been given. So, what in this experience was there to be grateful for? My family! As hard as it was for me to stay in that long brick building far away from them, it must have been doubly hard for them to follow the advice of the "experts" and leave me there. How much they sacrificed to make the 200-mile round trip every single Sunday just to be with me for three hours! Even on Thanksgiving, when we could leave only for the day, my parents would pick me up early in the morning and drive home with me while Annie cooked Thanksgiving dinner. I would spend a few precious hours eating lunch and visiting with my family before having to return to that long brick building by the witching hour of 4:00. My parents drove 400 miles every Thanksgiving day for four years just so I could celebrate the day with them. If that isn't love, what is?

A Child's Answered Prayer

I wheeled over to the chart on the wall in the main hall of that long brick building where I had spent the last four years. I was checking to see if my name had been added to the list of children who would be "going home for good" at the end of the quarter. Even though I prayed every night for my name to appear on that list, it wasn't there yet.

I was eight years old then, old enough to have the routine ingrained in me. I'd come to measure my life by quarters, those three-month spans of time that culminated with a vacation at home. We were allowed to spend one glorious week at home at the end of March, two heavenly weeks at the end of June, one delightful week at the end of September, and two magical weeks at Christmas. There was no joy greater than going home and no sadness worse than coming back. Often after returning to that place, I would dream that I was back at home, only to awaken and see the stark walls and feel the barrenness around me.

The one figure that made life bearable for me at the institution during that time was Ginny. She and I were roommates at the hospital school for two quarters. For one of those quarters, we were fortunate enough to have a room all by ourselves – just the two of us. Ginny was a few years older than I, making her like a big sister to me. Ginny was there at the long brick building, not because she had cerebral palsy, but because she'd had polio and had to have hip surgery that required her to be in a full body cast and lie flat of her back for a few months. While I was bound to a wheelchair, Ginny was bound to a stretcher.

Ginny and I shared much more than a room together. We shared our hurts, our dreams, our hopes. One night we decided to pray really hard that the next morning she would wake up without her body cast and I would wake up able to walk. Although those fervent wishes didn't come true, it felt good to have someone to share a childish hope with. Day after day, we played Barbie dolls together and talked for hours on end. Ginny was the one who took my leg braces off for me at the end of the day and gently rubbed baby oil on my heel where the braces had blistered it.

Ginny's home town was only about 15 miles from mine, so she visited me during our vacations at home. Before our last vacation, Ginny's name was on that savored list of children who would not be returning to the institution. Her body cast had been removed, and she could walk with her crutches again. Although I was happy for her, I couldn't bear the thought of being there at the long brick building without her. Another friend, Donnie, had already been sent home to go to a regular school. I would be left to endure the cruelty and loneliness all by myself.

It was March, so this break lasted only one precious week. I loved the beginning of the week and hated the end. I don't remember doing anything special during my brief time at home, just enjoying being with my family and my beloved new puppy Spot and going to the country to visit relatives on my Dad's side. Annie's home cooked meals were a welcome respite from the institutional food. And oh, how grand it was to be able to make choices – what I wanted to wear, what I wanted to watch on TV, what toys I wanted to play with. Best of all, though, was the reprieve from therapy, the wearing of braces, and the fear of reprisal for seemingly innocent acts that might irritate a tired and impatient house mother. So was spent a most delightful week at home.

Then all of a sudden it was there – the dreaded Sunday when it was time to go back. My little girl prayers had not been answered. I was devastated. I pleaded not to go, but my parents insisted that I must because there was no school at home that would take me.

Somehow I had to make them understand. This was more than just a little girl's preference to stay at home rather than go away to camp for a week. These emotions sprang from the very root of my being and surfaced in anguished, uncontrollable tears. Between sobs, I could say only, "I can't go back. I just can't." But the clock was ticking and the hour of departure was fast approaching. We were sitting in the living room, just my parents and I. How could I make them see? They hadn't been there, not in the midst of the grueling, painful therapy, not in the midst of the lonely nights and the house mothers bereft of all emotions. Those experiences defied the expressive abilities of an eight-year-old who had existed for four years in a sterile land where no adult actively sought conversation with the young inmates.

Finally I said it, not in eloquent words, but in words filled with indisputable resolve. "I can't stand it any more. I'll kill myself if you take me back." For a few minutes the room was quiet except for my sobbing. No one spoke. After what seemed like hours, Daddy said softly, "You don't have to go back." At long last the clock had stopped ticking, and there was nothing to dread any more. In a way I had never imagined, God had answered my prayer and let me go home for good.

Annie and Pappy

Pappy walked into Woolworth's Dime Store carrying me on one arm and leading Wanda by the other. He said, "Ok, girls, pick out anything you want and it's yours." That sums up my memory of my mother's parents, Annie and Pappy, who came to live with us when Wanda was born. My mother was an only child, making us Annie's and Pappy's only grandchildren. And to say they adored us was the greatest understatement of the century.

Pappy drove around in a little black pickup truck, usually with Wanda in tow. In fact, he took great pride in the fact that it was his job to take Wanda to school every morning and pick her up in the afternoon. When he wasn't on chauffeur duty, Pappy loved to go fishing with his sister and her husband. They often brought home long strings of fish from Grenada Lake.

Annie, on the other hand, was happy to stay on the home front and cook to her heart's content. Her foods were definitely comfort foods – biscuits, cornbread, turnip greens, fried apple pies, caramel pecan candy – the best that cooking had to offer. She never used a recipe; instead, she mixed her ingredients according to the way the food felt or looked. She could tell by the feel of the dough whether she had the right amount of shortening in her biscuits.

What did Annie and Pappy look like? Pappy was short for a man, but not pudgy by any means. Although as a young man he had black wavy hair, he later preferred to wear it cut very close, almost shaved. Pappy loved his moustache and groomed it impeccably. For his clothing, he preferred suspenders rather than a belt, and he sometimes wore overalls.

Annie was, for all my life, stooped, with her neck frozen in a downward position. She probably would have been a rather tall woman if she could have stood upright. Her hair was always gray, never white, and she kept it curled with a home permanent. Annie wore long-sleeved cotton dresses to hide the psoriasis that covered her arms and legs. She always had an apron tied around her waist; that seemed to mark her identity. The only piece of jewelry she ever wore was a clover leaf pin I gave her one Mother's Day.

Since I was unable to sit alone in my early childhood, Annie held me in her lap for the better part of my first four years. She read to Wanda and me by the hour, moving her finger along the words. To Annie's credit, I was able to read by the time I was four years old.

When Annie wasn't holding me, she was cooking or ironing. Oddly enough, though, it was Pappy who potty trained me.

When I left home at age four to stay at the long brick building, Annie and Pappy came with my parents and Wanda to see me every Sunday. Knowing how much I liked Coke, Pappy was delighted when a Coke machine was installed in the building and I was allowed to buy one Coke a day. In those days a Coke cost a dime, so every Sunday Daddy and Pappy filled my coin purse with dimes. I have no doubt that I had more dimes than even the staff. During that time, Annie often made tins of her caramel pecan candy to give to the staff, probably in hopes of "bribing" them into being kind to me.

As evident from the beginning of this chapter, what I remember most about Annie and Pappy is that they would have given Wanda and me the moon if they could somehow have climbed that high. I don't remember either of them ever saying "no" to a single one of our requests. In fact, one September at the end of one of my vacations at home, I told Pappy I wanted a watermelon. Well, my "wants" weren't in sync with the seasons, and watermelons were pretty scarce in September. Undaunted, Pappy rode around with me in the truck until we found a watermelon – no matter that it cost four times the usual price.

By the time I came home, we had gotten a little puppy named Spot. Annie gave Spot a bath every Saturday before they came to see me on Sunday. She fed Spot with a spoon and rocked him to sleep in her lap before laying him in a doll crib. We were never quite successful at house training Spot, so Annie, not wanting Spot to get in trouble, got up early every morning before anyone else and mopped the kitchen floor. Imagine that – stooped from the neck down and still mopping a massive size kitchen.

As Annie grew older and even more stooped, there was only one chair that was comfortable for her. It was a large recliner in the den right in front of the television. Spot usually lay in the chair beside her, with his little head on the

armrest. I often sat in my wheelchair beside her recliner and watched the television shows that we both liked.

In her later years, Annie still tried to cook some, but she ate very little of what she cooked. Her diet was so simple and so limited that it became etched in my memory. For breakfast she wanted only buttered bread (not toasted), a banana, milk, and coffee. Her lunch consisted of boiled chicken, "new potatoes," green beans, and ice cream. At night she ate peanut butter and crackers, a banana, and ice cream. It made no difference what we ate or what we offered her; she had created her own diet and she would not deviate from it.

Although Annie must surely have been in pain, she took only liquid Tylenol – nothing more to ease the pain. And whatever pain she suffered evidently stayed between her and God, because she never spoke of it. Gradually she spent less time in the kitchen, and most afternoons she spent reading the newspaper in bed. People who came to visit Annie had to kneel in front of her chair so she could see their faces.

One May evening in 1981, Annie sustained a fall that we later learned was caused by a stroke. She died less than 24 hours later. She was 84, and I was 25. Annie and Pappy had been married 66 years.

Pappy lived six years after Annie died. A gregarious fellow, Pappy talked to anyone and everyone who would talk to him. His greatest enjoyment was going to get coffee every morning with his postman friend.

Pappy continued his giving spirit, often leaving a quarter on top of the outdoor trash cans for the trash collectors. Pappy loved company, and it was his trademark to give every visitor something – a pack of razor blades, a package of chewing tobacco (whether they chewed or not), a calendar, anything that he thought would remind them to come back. In fact, Pappy kept a record of his visitors, and anyone who didn't come to see him within the time he thought proper was blackballed from his list of pallbearers!

Pappy lived long enough for us to tell him that Wanda (he called her "Little Bit") was going to have a baby (we couldn't use the word "pregnant" in his presence). But in March before Avent was born in August, Pappy had to have emergency surgery for a blockage that turned out to be colon cancer. Even though the surgery was radical, there were a couple of days when we thought he might recover. If he did live, he would need nursing home care. He had always said, "To hell with a nursing home." Although we didn't tell him that was in the works, he probably sensed it. Pappy had always said, too, that he wanted to die with his shoes on. He almost did. Only six days after his surgery, he passed away. He was 90, and I was 31.

From childhood, I can remember hearing Annie and Pappy each praying late at night in a low voice, "Please let little Maxine be able to walk." Even though they didn't see those prayers answered on this earth, I have no doubt that they'll see them answered when we're together again in heaven.

A psychologist friend of mine once told me that all children need someone in their lives other than their parents who think that child is the most wonderful human being on the planet. Annie and Pappy were those "someones" to Wanda and me.

Annie's Letters

Every letter began the same way: "Dear sweet, smart Maxine." And day after day they came – Tuesday through Saturday, for more than four years – the entire time I was away from home at the long brick building.

Annie wrote the letters, every one of them, on lined tablet paper in her large but clear handwriting. She told of happenings back home – about visits from Aunt Coot and Uncle Otis, about fish that Pappy had caught in Grenada Lake, and about vegetables she had put in the freezer from the gardens of family and friends.

When I was still very young, a house mother would read the letters to me, but pretty soon I was able to read them myself. Oh, the worth of those letters! Today I remember her words "Dear sweet, smart Maxine." I must have heard or read those same words almost 1,000 times over the course of those four years. There is no doubt that they helped me believe I had value. I sensed the therapists' disapproval with me for making no real strides in learning to walk, and I felt the house mothers growing impatient because I continued to need help eating and dressing. But I always knew that Annie loved me no less because I couldn't walk, Annie believed in me no less because I couldn't use my hands; she simply treasured me for who I was, and she asked for nothing more. She gave me the gift of learning to accept myself.

Annie had little formal education herself, but what she taught me was priceless.

The Lady with the Wings

As we sat and talked in my living room one afternoon not so long ago, I suddenly knew that this chapter about my first encounter with Mem would be titled "The Lady with the Wings." Memories came flooding back of my first day with her as my teacher.

I had just turned nine years old and had just come home a few months earlier from the residential facility where I felt like a prisoner. Now I desperately wanted to go to "real" school in my home town. My sister attended a beautiful brick elementary school at the end of a stately, tree-lined boulevard near our home. Every time we passed by, I would say, "I want to go to school there." But my parents had already approached the principal on this topic, and his response was "It just won't work." Regular schools were made for regular children, those whose legs walked, whose hands wrote, and whose speech was unbroken. I didn't fit that description.

The only school open to me was the Leflore County School for Handicapped Children, nicknamed the Little Red School. There, school days lasted only from 8:30 until 11:30, and most of the students who attended had intellectual impairments that caused them to be unable to keep up academically with their age peers. Still, it was school, and it was an opportunity for me to learn. That first morning, my mother drove me to school, pulled my wheelchair out of the car, and set me in it. The adult size chair swallowed my tiny frame, and my pony tail barely hung out over the back. Mama rolled me down the sidewalk toward the red brick building that was once school to first graders. Now it served children who weren't in any grade.

The school's director and head teacher was Mrs. Mary Elizabeth Morton ("Mem"). When I met Mrs. Morton, her beauty was striking to me. She had kind eyes and a wide and gentle smile, and her hair was ever so neatly coiled on top of her head in a bun. She had a magical personality that lit up the whole room; and when she talked, her hands fluttered with expression.

Though Mrs. Morton taught me many things over the years, I think I learned my most important lesson that first day – a lesson about respect and understanding. There was another student with cerebral palsy in my class. Her name was Martha, and her disability was more severe than mine. Although she couldn't speak, I watched as she communicated with her eyes. At one point, Martha nodded toward her seat and looked up at Mrs. Morton, who smiled knowingly and asked, "Do you need me to rest you a little?" This routine was obviously familiar to both of them. Wheelchair-bound, Martha sat in heavy metal braces up to her waist, and the constant pressure on her seat soon gave way to pain. Mrs. Morton knew what to do to relieve the pressure. She reached behind Martha, grasped the braces on each side, lifted Martha up and held her suspended for a few moments, then lowered her back into the chair. Martha gave a look that meant "Thank you"; and Mrs. Morton acknowledged it with a smile.

Though I felt encouraged by the attitudes in this new school, my previous experiences still gave me cause to distrust any and all caregivers outside my own family. And so it was with much apprehension that I finally asked Mrs. Morton to do for me that most horrid of all tasks -- take me to the bathroom. "Okey doke," she responded, as though it were no big deal. She wheeled me into the stall and gently but confidently lifted me onto the seat, in the same way my mother did. I sat and sat, all the while thinking to myself, "I must go ... I must. She'll be so angry if I've asked to go and now I can't." But the more anxious I became and the harder I tried, the more my body resisted. Terror-stricken, I finally looked up at her and said in a very small voice, "I really thought I needed to go, but I can't." I was fully prepared for a thorough scolding. Instead, Mrs. Morton smiled at me and said, "It's all right. That happens to all of us sometimes." Oh, how profound the relief! How welcome this new teacher – this "Lady with the Wings"!

Rachel and Bert

Rachel and Bert – they were the two precious children of two precious people. And though Rachel and Bert were on this earth for only a brief time, they left a powerful influence that will live forever. You see, children who help us to see what love really is stay with us for all time.

Rachel was born before I ever came to know her parents, Mem and Bobby. She died in infancy, so I met her only through the smiling eyes and gentle voice of her mother and through the tender hug and soft laugh of her father.

I met Rachel's brother, Bert, when I was about 9 and he was 10 or 11. His mother Mem, was the director of the day school I attended. She was also my primary teacher at "Little Red," as the school was fondly called. Bert was a student there, too. I can still picture him sitting on his mother's lap, his feet touching the floor. I remember how much Bert liked Christmas trees – so much that Mem and Bobby began putting live trees up early in December, for his birthday on December 3rd. Live trees didn't last long, so they kept replacing them with fresh ones. How glad they were when artificial trees came along, for then Bert could have a Christmas tree in his room all year. Somehow, I remember all the ways they told him, "I love you," and I remember how it didn't matter that he couldn't speak those words back to them.

Bert died at age 13. A child myself, I remember only the sadness I felt in knowing that Mem and Bobby, people I loved, were hurting. Only in adulthood did I understand both their loss and their gain. I came to realize that losing a child is the most heart-wrenching experience anyone ever faces. I came to realize, too, that children have a special love that lives on forever in the hearts of those who have known them and in the lives that are forever touched by their innocence and goodness.

Mem and Bobby have spent the rest of their lives caring for others who needed them – me included. When I was a child, they gave me back the dignity that the residential facility had tried to strip away. Bobby, a farmer, often came to the school during the winter months to play with us kids. He laughed so hard every time I beat him at double-nine dominoes. Mem always praised me for my academic prowess. As an adult, it has been a blessing to have their friendship and their continued interest in all aspects of my life.

Today I think of Rachel and Bert when Mem calls me "Darlin'" and when Bobby gives me a bear hug. I love the heart-eyes that Mem and Bobby see with. Heart-eyes look past human frailties and look straight into human goodness and value. Heart-eyes find the gold that's hidden inside broken bodies.

My Wings of Opportunity

The day began as any other day at Little Red had, except that this was the last day of my third year as a student there. Little did I know that it would be my very last day as a student in a school for children with disabilities.

I sensed something different that morning. My mother took me to school as usual; but instead of leaving right away, she lingered, making small talk with another mother. Soon Mrs. Morton came and stood close, very close beside me. She wanted to tell me something. Slowly, carefully, she explained that next year I would be going to school with my sister and all the other children in my neighborhood. The doors to that candy store school had been unlocked, and I had been invited to come in! I could scarcely believe what I was hearing. Questions whirled from my mouth. "How will I get to my classes?" "How will I take my tests?" Those were the spoken questions. But there were others that could not be spoken. "What will the other children (and the teachers) think of me?" "Will I be smart enough to keep up?"

In her gentle manner that was now so familiar to me, Mrs. Morton reassured me that everything would be just fine. The other students would push my wheelchair from one class to another, and I would type my lessons on an electric typewriter, also on wheels. Yes, everything would be fine, because Mrs. Morton had paved the way for me. Everything would be fine, because Mrs. Morton had believed in me enough to teach me.

When I came to Little Red at age 9, Mrs. Morton wasted no time in beginning my education. In keeping with my age, she gave me fourth grade books to study. The only exception was math. This was the period in education when "arithmetic" changed to "the new math" and the whole approach to teaching and learning the rules of numbers changed. Rather than make a sudden switch, Mrs. Morton started from the beginning, with first grade workbooks. We flew through the early, easy parts, often working ten pages of problems at a time. But we did every one, not skipping over a single concept. In three years, we waded through five grades of math workbooks, until I reached grade level knowing "the new math."

Most importantly, Mrs. Morton saw potential in a little girl swallowed up by a wheelchair – a little girl whose greatest dream was just to go to "regular school." So it happened that when a new principal, Mr. Waits, came to the public school in our neighborhood (the school where I had been denied entrance), and when he and his family moved next door to us and came to know me, Mrs. Morton saw this as her chance to help me enter a world that I'd only looked at longingly, as a child looks through the window of a candy store but is not allowed to go in.

Sharing my dream, Mrs. Morton went to Mr. Waits with her conviction that I could succeed in a regular school. Would he agree? If Mr. Waits opened his school to me, he would be putting his career on the line. In the 1960s, children with disabilities as severe as mine were typically excluded from regular schools. Would Mr. Waits go against the tide of the times and give me a chance? Yes! With a big heart and an open mind, he opened the doors of Bankston Elementary School to me.

Was it a coincidence that Mr. Waits became principal when I needed a man like him who cared more about the future of that one child in a wheelchair than about preserving the status quo? Was it a coincidence that Mr. Waits and his family moved next door to us and got to know me as an ordinary little girl with a ponytail? Was it a coincidence that Mr. Waits served as principal for only three years – one year to become my friend, one year to give me my chance, and one year to be sure that the junior high principal gave me a chance, too? Or were those God-incidences? And were Mrs. Morton and Mr. Waits put in my path for just such a time as this? You decide.

My conviction is that God sent Mrs. Morton and Mr. Waits into my life to give me the future He wanted me to have. No, they couldn't give me my legs, but they did give me my wings.

The Joys of Regular School

To say I was excited that first day at Bankston Elementary School would be a huge understatement. To say I was nervous would also be an understatement. After all, I was 12 years old, going to a regular school for the first time in my life. It felt funny. I was finally going through the doors of that school I had looked at so wistfully, so longingly, for three years. But now that my mother was rolling me down the long hall, I found I didn't know what to expect. Would they laugh? Would they stare? Or would they simply ignore me?

To my great delight, they smiled. They spoke to me and welcomed me. "Hi, Maxine," I heard as I made my way to my homeroom. I learned later – much later – that the principal (Mr. Waits) and the teachers had prepared the students for my arrival. These wise adults had paved the way for me by explaining to the students that a new classmate would be arriving who needed their help because even though she could learn just fine, she couldn't walk, nor could she use her hands very well. Mr. Waits and the teachers also explained that my speech would be a little different, but that they could understand me if they really listened.

When I arrived at my homeroom, my teacher, Mrs. Deaton, was there waiting. She looked lovely to me, with her hair beautifully coifed and her suit perfectly tailored. She smiled softly and invited me to go in early and get settled before the bell rang. Inside the classroom were five rows of desks, but none was mine. I couldn't sit in a desk, so my mother parked my wheelchair in the back of the room near a long counter that would easily accommodate my books. In a few weeks I would have my electric typewriter on a rolling table. Then I could write just like everyone else, almost.

My mother arranged my books on the counter, patted me on the shoulder, and quietly left the room. As I waited for the bell to ring and the other students

to come in, I looked out the long row of windows and wondered what this day would bring. I remember praying silently, "Well, it's just you and me now, God."

Finally the bell rang and the other 25 or so students filed in. Everything was new to me but not to them. Mrs. Deaton stood before the class and led the Pledge of Allegiance. I was happy that I knew the words. The next series of events that opened the school day forced me to pay careful attention. "How many of you are not eating in the cafeteria today?" asked Mrs. Deaton. I didn't raise my hand. I would be eating in the cafeteria, that day anyway.

We had reading and spelling in homeroom. Then, instead of changing classes with my homeroom, I stayed in the same class for English. When it was time for social studies, a classmate wheeled me down the hall. As strange as it sounds, even this bit of normality brought me incredible delight.

At lunch time my mother came to help me eat. The cafeteria was filled with children from all grades. Many from the lower grades looked at me a little curiously, especially when my mother began feeding me. I'm sure they had never seen anyone my age being fed. I felt uncomfortable and ate very little. We learned that some of the children went home for lunch, so my mother began taking me home at lunch time and bringing me back for my afternoon classes.

Science was my first class after lunch, and Mrs. Jarman was my teacher. She was a tall lady with a motherly smile. I remember loving the way she taught us how the parts of the body work. It made me wish I could become a doctor.

My last class of the afternoon was math. I can still see Mrs. Tubbs standing before us in her suit and high-heeled shoes. She was short in stature but long in her enthusiasm for teaching math. She was always ready with a word of praise.

Though I made good grades, the question continued to haunt me: "Can I keep up with the other students?" I was frightened of being taken out of this school I loved so much if I didn't perform well. To my great joy and relief, my first report card brought all A's!

Each day, my classmates wheeled me with my rolling typewriter from one class to another. My typewriter had a special keyguard to keep me from striking several keys at once. As other students wrote, I typed, one precious key at a time. My typing was painfully slow – maybe 6 to 8 words a minute, but I was determined to finish my classwork before I left school, even if it meant holding up the entire carpool line!

Though neither my teachers nor my fellow students had any experience with children like me, they accepted me with kindness, patience, and understanding. There were certain students who always "took care of me"; and all those Dee Dee's, Cathy's, and Patsy's (you know who you are) will always have a special place in my heart.

Simple things like taking the day's absences to the office and being the referee during games of touch football at recess brought me such delight. I was included in every activity, even my homeroom class play, in which I played a gray-haired lady at Tom Sawyer's funeral. My teacher had wisely asked me what kind of part I would feel comfortable with. "A part that doesn't require speaking will be fine," I told her. Though I loved talking with my friends, I thought my speech was too different to take the spotlight before an audience.

Apparently my singing ability was too different for chorus, too. One day in music class the teacher ordered us to line up beside the piano for chorus tryouts. My friends, wonderfully accustomed to taking me with them, dutifully wheeled me into the line. When I reached the piano, the teacher frowned and said to my little friend, "Take her back. She can't sing." I was far more embarrassed for my friend than for myself.

Fortunately, I was more gifted academically than musically. My classmates soon became aware of my academic prowess, and one day they seized an opportunity to make good use of it. We were taking a true-false test, dictated orally by the teacher. After each question, I typed "true" or "false." The teacher smelled a rat when she noticed that the other students were waiting to write their answers until I had finished typing mine. They were counting my keystrokes! Their fun ended, though, when the teacher came to me and whispered, "Just type T or F."

I continued to make good grades, but I had to study hard. If I needed extra time to complete a test or other class work, my teachers gladly obliged. At night, my mother spent hours writing homework assignments as I dictated them to her. Little by little, my confidence mounted, and I began to feel at home in that candy store I was finally allowed to enter.

Awards Day

I relived that day a hundred times in my mind. So great was my joy that I wanted to experience it over and over. I wanted to dwell on each moment, to savor it and somehow preserve it so that its imprint would never fade.

It was Awards Day at the elementary school I attended. Even though I was in the sixth grade, this was my first time ever to attend Awards Day; indeed, this was my first year in a school with children who were considered "normal" – that is, who had no disabilities. My disability was all too evident – the cerebral palsy that had gripped me from birth stole from me the ability to make my limbs do my bidding and the ability to speak clearly and without effort. But I refused to let it steal my spirit. Today was proof of that.

I wore a pink skirt that day, and my ponytail, as usual, hung over the back of my wheelchair. Waiting in line with the rest of my class to enter the auditorium, I watched as the students filed by the principal, Mr. Waits. Suddenly, out of the corner of my eye, I caught a glimpse of Mem; then she disappeared. She was obviously trying to avoid letting me see her. "What's she doing here?" I wondered. My heart skipped a beat as I realized that something special was about to happen.

A classmate pushed my chair to the doorway of the auditorium; then my homeroom teacher, Mrs. Deaton, gently backed my chair down the single step and parked me in front of the first row of seats. It always thrilled me to go to the auditorium – to see the large stage with the heavy curtain and the flags standing tall, and to hear the rustle of people in the audience. Today there were parents as well as students in the assembly. I looked toward the back, where the parents were sitting; and sure enough, there was Mama. Another sign that today was special.

Did I dare hope to receive an award? I couldn't let myself even think about that. After all, it was only a year ago that I had worried so about not being able to keep up with the other students. True enough, I had done well – very well – in my classes, but how could it be possible that I would be worthy of recognition in this, my first year? Still, my heart raced, and anticipation swept over me.

Mr. Waits stood in front of the stage, greeted those assembled, and began to call the names of students receiving awards. In my grade an award was given in each subject to the student with the highest average in that subject. I clapped as students I knew received awards in math, science, and social studies. Then suddenly I heard, "And the English award goes to Maxine Harper."

The students went wild with applause, and the parents followed suit. Some parents, seeing no child standing, wondered who this new name, never before heard on Awards Day, belonged to. Then they saw me, sitting in my wheelchair, as Mr. Waits placed the medal in my hands. Applause filled the auditorium as children, parents, and teachers gave me a standing ovation. The joy that rose up within me was indescribable. If that weren't enough, though, I received yet another award – the Literary Award for the best book report. The applause broke forth again, and my heart nearly burst as I realized that so many shared my joy.

After the assembly I received a multitude of hugs and congratulations. The rest of the day was filled with festivities – picture-taking, parties, even a street dance that night. All the things I'd dreamed of being a part of had now become my new reality – my new life.

Spot

It was an ordinary Sunday in early December 1963, much like other Sundays during my stay at the residential facility. At straight up 1 o'clock, my family had picked me up from the long brick building, and we had gone to spend the afternoon with my cousin Mett and Aunt Colie, who lived in the area. Daddy carried me into their small living room and set me on the sofa.

After our usual greeting, Mett slipped into the back of the house and came out with a small bundle of fur wrapped in a towel. She laid it in my lap, and I gazed at it with wide-eyed amazement. Here was the puppy I had been begging for. He was ever so tiny – only about three weeks old, legs still wobbly, and eyes barely open. He was white with a few black spots, so I thought he had to be named Spot. Whoever coined the phrase "mixed breed" must have had Spot in mind. Picture a combination of a wire-haired Chihuahua with black muscadine eyes on stems, a terrier with pointed ears and a long white tail that arched over his back, and a feisty personality, and there you have Spot.

Spot lay contentedly in my lap for the rest of the afternoon. I couldn't take my eyes off him. The bonding between Spot and me was immediate and unquestionable. It was harder than ever to leave my family that Sunday because I was leaving Spot, too.

Every Sunday from then on, Spot came with my family to see me. He would sleep all the way, until they were within a few blocks of that long brick building; then he would wake up and scratch at the windows until I got to the car. When we were together again at last, his joy was evident in the wild wagging of his tail and the nuzzling of his head against my neck. He cut his teeth chewing on my finger.

That first Christmas we put a tiny red turtleneck sweater on Spot. As he pranced around in it, we roared with laughter. That was the first of many doggie clothes he wore. Through the years we dressed him in a plaid jacket, a clip-on bow tie, and a rhinestone collar. He loved it all.

I finally came home when Spot was about four months old. At last we were together, with no more separations. He found his "place" right under my wheelchair, where he would sit and peek out and dare anyone to come close. He loved riding around the neighborhood with Wanda and me in the golf cart Daddy had bought for us. Spot even knew that the accelerator made it go, and he would paw at it when we stopped. Spot liked my grandmother's cooking as much as we did, and she purposefully cooked foods he liked, such as fried chicken, liver and onions, mashed potatoes, and black-eyed peas.

When I came home from school in the afternoons, I would sit at the typewriter for hours doing homework. Spot lay beside me ever so patiently, not moving until I did. At supper time he would follow me to the kitchen, wait there until he heard the sound of the straw at the bottom of the glass, then run to follow me back to the typewriter. He assigned himself the role of being my companion and protector, and nothing could dissuade him from that. I'm certain that he sensed my need for his love, and he gave it wholeheartedly. I don't use the word "wholehearted" lightly; he actually loved me and me alone. He liked a few people and tolerated others, but I was the object of his full adoration.

When Spot was about 6 years old, I almost lost him when a German shepherd jumped him in the front yard. The big dog's mouth engulfed Spot's middle, and his fangs pierced him through. He spent a week at the vet's while we prayed that he would survive. Then very early on Saturday morning, I went into the kitchen to find that Daddy had brought Spot home. We immediately went into our hugging mode. I would wheel up beside the large recliner in the den, and Spot would stand in the recliner with his front feet on the armrest and nuzzle my neck while I wrapped my arm around him and held him close.

The years passed. I grew up and Spot grew old. When he was about 16, we noticed that he was having trouble jumping into the chair. The vet laughed when we asked him about it. "He is 16, you know." But he's supposed to live forever! My mind knew better, but my heart refused to believe otherwise.

Even though Spot had always been cold natured, he grew even more so in his old age. I began to get up several times during the night to cover him up in his little bed in the kitchen. I always sat with him until he stopped shivering. Then one night shortly before his 19th birthday, I got up to check on him and found him whimpering, obviously in pain. I sat with him the rest of the night. The next day the vet said he had an intestinal blockage. There was nothing he could do except give him pain shots. I wanted him to die peacefully in his sleep, but he was a feisty little fellow and he would have none of that. Finally I knew I had to let my Spot go. Daddy picked him up in his little bed and laid him across my chair. I kissed him gently and said, "I'm sending you back to the One who sent you to me."

High School Graduation

It began as just another day of my senior year at Pillow Academy. I had spent my high school years there, with many of the same friends who had heralded my entrance into "regular" school. We were a pretty close knit group of 107 seniors preparing to don caps and gowns and march across the football field to receive our diplomas. There were three Harper girls in the same graduating class – Wanda, our cousin Lisa, and myself.

It was May, and the graduation excitement was mounting. This day was unusually warm; and although the pants suit I wore was one of my favorites, I was drenched with perspiration by the time my classes were over.

My mother wheeled me outside, up the ramp and into the van. She had just closed the double side doors when suddenly the school secretary came running out. "Mrs. Harper," she said, "Mr. Carothers would like to see you." Without hesitation, my mother went in to see the headmaster, leaving me in the van to wonder what he had to say. My curiosity began to run high. As I waited, with the hot sun pouring through the windows, my mind rummaged quickly over the past days wondering what error I had committed.

Finally, after what seemed like hours, my mother and the secretary emerged from the building. I noticed with a start that there were tears in their eyes. Following close behind was Mr. Carothers. Reaching the van, he flung open the side doors so that he could see me. Always a kindly man, he seemed that day to have an extra sparkle to his kindness. I could see the joy in his face as he told me that grades had been averaged and I was the valedictorian of the Class of 1974!

I wish there were words to express the joy that was in my heart at that moment, but no words are adequate. I had come from the depths of a residential facility through the valley of struggles and up to the mountaintop of success for a high school senior. Perhaps it was the valleys that made the mountaintop seem so high.

Looking back on my valedictory address some 35 years later, I'm somewhat amazed by the message it speaks to me. It concluded with these words:

As we look now to our future, we realize that the road ahead may not always be an easy one. But let us remember that obstacles do not have to signal defeat; they can be used to achieve an even greater victory. This is dependent, however, to a great extent upon how we accept life. Our class motto, written by Henry Ward Beecher, states, "God asks no man whether he will accept life. That is not the choice; you must take it. The only choice is how."

The attitude with which we accept life is a vital key in determining the ultimate impact of our lives. Therefore, let us take life with eagerness and with a determination to use it to the fullest. Our talents should not be buried, but should be used to benefit ourselves and others; for in helping our fellow man, we enrich our own lives as well.

Finally, we must not be afraid to dream. Untold accomplishments can be ours if we make our dreams worthwhile ones and if we are willing and determined to persevere in those dreams and to see them through to fruition.

Life is a gift, an opportunity, a challenge. Let us, with the help of God, fulfill that wonderful challenge.

Pillow valedictorian gets standing ovation

Maxine Harper, daughter of Mr. and Mrs. Max A. Harper was elected valedictorian of the 1974 Class of Pillow Academy. Her average was 98.428. Miss Harper received a standing ovation from the faculty and students when the announcement was made.

The popular coed will continue her studies at Mississippi Delta Junior College.

Named salutatorian was Ann Rutledge, daughter of Mr. and Mrs. J. M. Rutledge. Her average was 98.294.

Miss Rutledge is serving as secretary of the senior class, treasurer of the student council, and is editor of the school newspaper.

During the 1973-74 school year she was president of the Mississippi Private School Honor Society and secretary of the Academy Press Association.

She was selected a National Merit Finalist and is named in Who's Who in American High Schools.

Miss Rutledge has served on the Pep Squad, Math Club, Y-Teens, Science Club, Photography Club, honor society, Latin Club and Crown Club.

She is a member of the First Baptist Church where she is president of the youth council and sings in the youth choir.

The salutatorian plans to continue her studies at Mississippi College, majoring in education.

Miss Harper has received outstanding awards in Latin I, World history, biology, English III, geometry, U.S. government and English IV. She was presented the Daughters of American Revolution history silver medal and was named one of the Altrusa Club's Girl of the Month.

MAXINE HARPER
Valedictorian

ANN RUTLEDGE
Salutatorian

College Years

College was difficult at first, not so much academically as emotionally and logistically. It's supposed to be a time for leaving the nest and spreading your wings. But that's hard to do when your wings are broken.

The friends with whom I had gone through high school were scattering in all directions, leaving me feeling empty and lonely. I watched enviously as Wanda and my friends excitedly prepared for dorm life. For graduation gifts, they had received luggage, towels, and other necessities for living away from home. I, on the other hand, had received necklaces, cologne, and other gifts that, while appreciated, reminded me that I would continue living at home with my parents. When I went with Mama and Daddy to move Wanda into the dorm, the tears I cried upon leaving her were not only tears of separation but also tears of grief for a life I could not have.

For my freshman year, I decided to attend a nearby community college. Even though I had graduated as valedictorian of my high school class, the college's Dean of Student Affairs wasn't convinced that I was college material. Sitting behind his big, distinguished looking desk, he muttered to me, "I'm not sure you can handle college, but we'll let you give it a try anyway."

As it turned out, the classes were far easier than my high school classes had been. In fact, my English comp teacher, Mrs. Shuttleworth, whom I thoroughly adored, pulled me aside after class one day and said, "I wanted to tell you that you are actually too advanced for this class, and I feel badly that you have to take it, but it's a required course." I liked to write, so I assured her that I didn't mind taking the class, that I actually enjoyed it.

I wasn't aware that Mrs. Shuttleworth was keeping some of my compositions and reading them to her classes as examples. Then one day years later, my second cousin, Michele, happened to be in Mrs. Shuttleworth's class when she read aloud an essay I had written about my aunt's house in the country. Michele recognized the description and immediately spoke up, "Hey, that's my grandmother's house!"

Since I was on campus at the community college only for classes, it was hard to make new friends. I was far removed from the revelry and camaraderie usually associated with the freshman year of college. It was a lonely year for me as I missed my high school friends.

For my sophomore year, I was ready to try commuting to Delta State University, 45 miles away. Needing drivers, I agreed to furnish the gasoline in exchange for having fellow commuters drive my van. I quickly had a van full of new friends. The joys of friendship began to return.

Having solved the problem of getting to school, I now had to find a way to get from one class to the next. I knew I couldn't rely on my voice, certainly not at first. So I decided to write a note to each of my teachers asking him/her to announce that I needed a ride to the next class from anyone who might be going in that direction. To this day, I remember the anxiety I felt, imagining that I might be stuck somewhere, unable to get to my next class. Of course, that never happened. I should have trusted God more.

One of the first people who volunteered to give me a ride was Allen. He was kind and compassionate, talking in a friendly manner as he wheeled me along. Somehow we discovered that we were distantly related. A few semesters later, his fiancée Reneé offered to give me a ride.

With some of my classes being on the second floor of buildings with no elevator, I had to be carried up and down the stairs. I always tried to make eye contact with the big, husky guys instead of the small, lean ones. After all, I did want to survive college!

My choice of a major was special education. My mother says that I'm a "natural-born teacher," and I wanted to make a difference in children's lives as Mem had done for me. I took all the required coursework for my major, including Art 101 and Speech 101. I hoped those two courses would not wreck my GPA.

The art course took tons of time even though the final products didn't show it. I painted on canvas until my knuckles bled. We did some painting in class so the teacher could give us pointers. One day I had yellow paint on my brush; and when Mr. Lester walked down my aisle, my hand got away from me and flung a yellow swatch on his favorite green sweater. It's a miracle he let me stay in his class. The only project in which I felt any sense of pride was an eight-block gray scale. Our assignment was to paint eight squares beginning with white and ending with black, in increments of gray such that the transition from one square to the next wasn't noticeable. I worked and worked until I had it just right. Mr. Lester was pleased, and so was I.

The speech class scared the stew out of me. I took it during summer school to shorten the suffering time. Before each assigned speech, I would write the speech out and then practice saying it into a tape recorder. I was never pleased with the way it sounded. I dreaded each day when it was my turn to give a speech. Fortunately, the class was small and friendly. The instructor was a pretty solemn man but quite fair in his grading. His policy was to praise, then critique. I really don't recall what he praised me for, but more than likely it had to do with the content of my speeches, not the delivery. What I do recall distinctly is the critique he gave me most often: "You need to keep your head still when you're speaking." Oh, how I wished I could!

The semesters flew by. Early on, my carpool gang and I were able to get all of our classes in the mornings. That way, the restroom was no real issue. None of the stalls were handicapped accessible, but I could easily wait until we got home. In later semesters, I had afternoon classes on some days, and sometimes no girls were riding with me. At first I reasoned, "I'll just limit my fluid intake beginning the night before." So, on Sunday, Tuesday, and Thursday nights I drank little or nothing. But by midday on Mondays, Wednesdays, and Fridays, I was already anticipating a miserable afternoon. Finally, on one of those days, I met up with a friend in the hall. "Hey, Manelle," I said, "I'll give you anything if you'll help me with something."

"Sure," she said. "What do you need?"

"I need to go to the bathroom. I'll pay you anything." I was desperate.

She laughed. "You know I don't mind helping you. Let's go." After that, we decided on a meeting place, and she helped me every day.

The next semester Sue commuted with me. She was newly married, trying to finish college on very little money. The first day of classes, we went to McDonald's for lunch. Sue didn't order, though. "I don't have any money today," she said.

"Well, I'll make a deal with you," I said. "I'll buy your lunch if you'll feed me mine." She was even gracious enough to help me in the restroom. That reciprocal help became our everyday routine. I've thought of our unique arrangement many times, and for me it carries a special sweetness in that helping each other just became a part of our lives – a very good and happy part of our lives. (I'm certain I got the better end of that deal, though.)

The time came when I could go no further without being officially admitted into the teacher education program. Yet there was a stumbling block. Among the committee members was a single dissenting voice, one who said I could not teach. But that's what I wanted to do more than anything else. It wasn't just a whim; teaching was in my blood. My father's mother (Granny) had been a teacher before me, and several of my cousins were teachers as well. More than that, I had a love for learning that spilled over into a love for teaching. I knew what a tremendous impact my teachers had had on me, particularly those like Mem, who taught me to believe in myself. I wanted to do the same for other children. Yes, I knew the odds were not in my favor. My speech was halting; my hands didn't work well; and I couldn't walk. Still, in my heart I wanted to teach, and I sincerely believed I could. I especially believed I had something to offer children who had difficulty learning. So I endured being the object of discussion, the object of contention.

On that momentous day when the committee met to make its decision, I sat in the lobby of the education building and waited to learn the fate of my career. The longer the clock ticked, the more anxious I became. What if they said no? I wouldn't even think about that now. They just had to say yes. After what seemed like forever, Dr. Buckner, my advisor and major professor (who was pulling for me), emerged from the conference room. I took a deep breath and prepared myself for the verdict. She smiled and I knew the answer. I was in! My dream of becoming a teacher was coming true.

My period of student teaching was a huge success, largely due to the patience and kindness of two excellent supervising teachers who helped me figure out the strategies that would work best for me. I felt a bond with the students – a bond that came from overcoming obstacles, each in our own way but with each other's help.

I remember working with a student who had a learning disability in reading. He was 14 years old, very bright, but reading on about 3rd or 4th grade level. Because of the difference between his age and his reading level, there was very little appropriate reading material available for him. He was only too aware of his reading problems, as I discovered one day when I was helping him with his spelling words. One of the words on his list was "illiterate." When we read it together, he responded, "That's what I am, isn't it?" That simple statement broke my heart, and I vowed to do everything I could to raise his self-esteem. Part of my solution was to let him record his own stories, either true or fictional. I would then transcribe the words he had spoken and let him read them back. What a difference it made! He read much more fluently, recognizing words that were his own. Furthermore, he was reading content appropriate for his age, intelligence, and interest level. He felt happy, and I felt immense gratification that I could actually help someone else!

In May 1978, I wheeled across the stage and received a Bachelor of Science Degree in Education. Yes, I was happy – I had graduated from college and had become licensed as a teacher. Once again, with God and my family by my side, I had beaten the odds!

The Long Night

From my hospital window I could see the lights of Miami Beach. All during the night before my surgery, I lay in bed with my face to the window and watched those lights. I wanted the night to pass, but I didn't want morning to come. I feared the unknown, and that's what morning would bring.

As a 21-year-old, this was my first time as a patient in a hospital since I was born. Fear gripped me, lodged in my throat, and emerged as tiny whimpers. My body, normally tense from the spasticity that enslaved it, shook all the more from the sheer terror that swept over me.

Why was I having this surgery? It was certainly elective, experimental even. The neurosurgeon would implant a pacemaker in my brain, with a wire going down my neck and into a round metal receiver implanted in my chest. The device was supposed to ease the spasticity that made my limbs so rigid and my speech so strained. Although the surgeon had eliminated walking as a possibility, maybe, just maybe, I could use my hands to feed and dress myself; and maybe, just maybe, my speech would be clearer, less distorted. These were my hopes, but there were no guarantees. In fact, the surgery was new, and it had been performed mostly on children. It was a four-hour surgery, and there were the usual risks, as well as the not-so-usual risks associated with surgery that was still experimental.

I didn't really want to have the surgery, but neither did I want to face the adulthood I saw before me. It was one thing to be dependent as a child; it was another to be dependent as an adult. My life dreams were no different from those of other young women – I wanted a career, marriage, children. The only difference was my limited capacity to pursue those dreams. I saw this surgery as my one hope of becoming "well enough" to live the life I dreamed of.

The night dragged on. No matter how hard I tried, I could not sleep. I was too frightened. What if something went wrong? What if I incurred even more brain damage? I wanted desperately to back out, not go through with the surgery. But then I would be branded a coward, or so I thought. Equally as bad, I would never know if my life could have been different.

As these thoughts darted through my mind like sharp, piercing arrows, night finally turned to dawn. About 6:00 a.m., a male nurse came and gave me an antibiotic shot – a normal precaution before surgery, he said. Soon other nurses brought more shots – shots that were supposed to calm my apprehensions. Instead, they increased my anxiety, and I wept uncontrollably.

My family – Mama, Daddy, and Wanda – waited with me until the orderlies finally came and placed me on a gurney to transport me to the operating room. My parents and Wanda walked beside me to the elevator and watched as the heavy doors opened and then closed, taking me away into a world that they could not share.

The orderlies placed my gurney along the wall in a line of other gurneys, all waiting their turn to enter the operating room. No one seemed to notice that tears were streaming down my face. Finally my turn came, and I was wheeled under the bright lights. The anesthesiologist sat on a stool beside the operating table where the orderlies had laid me. He spoke kindly, saying he would deaden my hand before starting the IV that would put me to sleep.

I awoke with a sense of relief. It was over. The deed was done, and I was still alive. What's more, the pain wasn't unbearable. I survived the surgery and even learned from the physical therapist how to transfer myself to and from my wheelchair. There was a brief time when I believed the pacemaker might be working. But in reality the surgery changed nothing, and a year later the stimulator was turned off.

I remember returning to Miami Beach for a check-up and realizing the surgery had failed. That night I sat alone outside our hotel for a very long time and stared at the lights glimmering over the water. The tears I had held back for a very long time streamed down my face. How I wish I had known then what I know now – what 30 years of life as an adult have taught me:

> "If God brings you to it,
> He will bring you through it.
> Happy moments, praise God.
> Difficult moments, seek God.
> Quiet moments, worship God.
> Painful moments, trust God.
> Every moment, thank God."
> -- Author Unknown

Graduate School

"You'll need a power chair," said the vocational rehabilitation counselor at Mississippi State University, the graduate school I was visiting. I was getting ready to take the plunge – going to a university two hours from home. It was the summer of 1978, and I was still reeling from the neurosurgery I had had in March of that year.

The power chair was only the beginning of my needs. As it turned out, I also needed a huge fan. My dorm had yet to be air conditioned, and that fall had to be the hottest on record.

More than anything, though, I needed an attendant – someone to help me bathe, dress, and eat. A young lady named Pariya from Thailand became my primary helper. Morning wasn't her thing, though, so a couple of the dorm housekeepers took over the morning routine.

My first day with Pariya, I discovered that English wasn't her thing either. When we went to the cafeteria for lunch, I asked for corn. Pariya gave me a puzzled look and said. "What's corn?" That was my first sign that communication would be a challenging part of our relationship. Another sign of our communication differences came several weeks later when I brought to the dorm a tiny plant and placed it in the window sill. Upon seeing it, Pariya exclaimed, "Wow! A tree!"

Though very kind, Pariya wasn't what one would call Americanized. She didn't eat American foods; rice that she cooked herself was her staple. At meal time she fed me but never ate with me. This was somewhat awkward for me, as I preferred to eat with someone instead of just being fed. All of Pariya's friends were international students, none of whom I ever met. Pariya couldn't drive, so going out together was impossible. Unfortunately, she could only meet my caregiving needs.

Thank goodness for Cyndi! She was one of those special people with whom I formed an immediate bond. She was tall, with beautiful blond hair and a broad, sweet smile. We had the same major, so we had most of our classes together. We became fast friends and Cyndi began taking me places in her car.

On Halloween night we were riding around when Cyndi's car ran out of gas in a less than desirable neighborhood. Cyndi took my chair from her car, set it on the sidewalk and set me in it. Then she said "I'll be back in a minute. I'm going to get some gasoline in a can." The minutes seemed like hours as I waited for Cyndi to come back. Fortunately no one kidnapped me. Even if they had, I think they would have brought me right back!

Living in the dorm was a new and unique experience. The "handicapped dorm" happened to be a freshman dorm, so I was with students much younger than I. My dorm experience was less exciting than that of most students going away from home for the first time. On my first night in the dorm, I remember going to bed about 10 o'clock and then realizing that I was probably the only one in bed at that hour.

Since I had to have two wheelchairs (one power and one manual) and a typewriter, there wasn't enough space for a roommate, so I had a private room. I took a television and a refrigerator with me, so it was almost like having my own tiny apartment.

I rode to class in my power chair, even at night, and even in the worst of weather. It rained and rained and rained. I bought a white slicker, and when the downpours came, I put on my slicker and put my chair into high gear. As I raced to class and passed everyone on the way, I heard the other students say "There goes white lightning!" Unfortunately, umbrellas were not my friend. I tried holding one between my legs and driving my chair. It worked until the wind caught it and flipped it upside down. As I sat there getting drenched, I raised the flag of surrender and threw my umbrella down. Surely whoever picked it up would have better luck with it than I had.

The campus was spread out in all directions, and it usually took me about 15 minutes to get to class. Once I arrived at the building, I had to ride the elevator up to the classroom. The buttons outside the elevator were low enough for me to reach, but the ones inside were higher; so my technique was to get on the elevator and ride it until someone got on who could press the buttons for me.

I liked my classes and did well in them, which reinforced my belief that Special Education was the right major for me. I relied on friends in my classes to take notes for me. They placed carbon paper under their notebook paper and made copies of their own notes. Lucky for me, I always found a good note taker in my classes.

My favorite professor was Dr. Obringer, who himself had a mild form of cerebral palsy. He had a great sense of humor and described his driving as better than his walking. He invited Cyndi and me to his house for eggnog at Christmas, and I got to hold his two-year-old baby boy, who weighed about 40 pounds. Surprise!

I learned that graduate school involved much more written work than undergraduate school had required. It was difficult to keep up with all of the papers that had to be written. I was still using a typewriter for everything, and my typing was really slow. I was thankful for the weekends when I could go home and my mom would type for me.

My final hurdle was the master's comps. They were long essay questions that required most students to write for three days. I wasn't sure that I could type that long, so I requested to be allowed to have a scribe – someone to write the answers as I dictated them. The chair of the department decided that I should have to write my own comps just like everyone else, so I spent about 4 days typing 8 hours a day. At the end of the exam period, to say that I was exhausted was a drastic understatement.

I passed my comps with flying colors, though. Then, just before graduation, the department chair called me into her office. I went eagerly, expecting a pat on the back, a message of congratulations, a vote of confidence that I would do well in my chosen career. Instead, I heard the stern, foreboding words, "I want to warn you that it won't be easy for you to get a job."

I swallowed hard. "Nothing has ever been easy," I replied in a low voice. At that very moment, her expression changed. Her face mellowed, and it seemed like she wished she could take her words back. She spoke once more, this time more softly. "I suppose you're right – nothing has ever been easy for you, has it?" I shook my head quietly and wheeled out of her office.

But I have a feeling that she was applauding with everyone else when, in May 1979, I graduated with a Master's Degree in Special Education, a 4.0 GPA, and a standing ovation.

Teaching at Little Red

The call came unexpectedly. I had completed my Master's Degree and had been desperately seeking a teaching position, but nothing had opened for me. Then Fred called. Fred was the principal at the school we fondly called Little Red. It was school to about 30 children with a variety of needs. In fact, it was the school I attended before I was admitted to public school. Now Fred was inviting me to come back as a teacher. How thrilling it was to think that my dream of teaching was finally coming true!

Little Red was indeed a little red schoolhouse, very old but with character. There were three classrooms on each side of the set of restrooms. There was a tiny kitchen and a room with a bathtub, washer and dryer – not what you would expect in a typical school, but what we needed to meet the needs of our children. Outside there was a huge playground with swings, slides, and other equipment that might be considered standard, but ours was built to accommodate children with disabilities.

I found myself coming into a well-established family of teachers, with Fred leading the gang. Fred was a tall man with a contagious laugh. He was unassuming, a blue jeans sort of guy who loved to play with the kids. And the kids absolutely adored him, as did the teachers. There were six of us teachers – all females. At one point three of the teachers were pregnant at the same time, and I teased Fred by saying, "I think the only reason you hired me was because you knew I wouldn't get pregnant."

I was assigned to teach the highest functioning adolescent class. On the first day of school there were eight eager faces greeting me – four boys and four girls. I remember realizing immediately what individual personalities they had. Charles and Eddie were boyish, always scrapping with each other. Charles was tall and lanky, just like an adolescent boy. Eddie had a contagious, mischievous grin, dangerous to a new teacher who was prone to laugh at inopportune times. Ronnie, a rather handsome young man, was shy and quiet. Roger was tall and full of laughter, always having a joke to tell. Teresa, always smiling, was eager to please and just wanted to be near me. Lisa had absolutely beautiful brown hair, always immaculately cut. She used sign language to communicate, and she was thrilled when I learned right away to understand her signs. Every morning she came rushing into the room with her fingers moving quickly as she talked to me. Deanna and Tanya were typical adolescent girls – best friends. They loved to giggle and talk about boys.

Through the years, my class changed. Some students stayed with me; others graduated; and still others joined my class. Patricia was sweet and funny, winking her way out of trouble. Cedric was a charmer, with a sweet smile and a lovable hug. William stayed in his cocoon until we discovered what an incredible singing voice he had. Larry was personable and considerate beyond his years.

My students always loved helping me. It seemed that they were not accustomed to helping someone else; they had always been on the receiving end. Now they were helping me tie my shoes, write on the chalk board, put papers on the bulletin board, and run errands for me. One day they even got to watch as my tire was changed when I ran over a thumbtack and the tire went flat. After that, we had thumbtack patrol, and the children received a reward for every thumbtack they rescued. I saw their self-esteem grow to new heights as they realized that they could do things that their teacher couldn't do. In fact, one mother confessed that this was her child's first year in this school and the first year that she had not cried every day. Knowing that boosted my own self-esteem as well.

Academically, we worked on skills that would help my students in the real world. They learned to write their name, address, and phone number. They learned to read a calendar, tell time, and count money. They even learned to use a calculator. In reading we focused on words they would see every day, like "stop, men, women, enter, exit." Normally, we worked at a long wooden table, with me sitting at the end and the students around the sides. They seemed to always want to be near me, and Fred began calling me "Mother Hen."

My students and I did many other fun activities together, including cooking meals in the tiny kitchen. Even though I couldn't cook, I showed my students how to make Kool-Aid, sandwiches, cookies, and even spaghetti. We also took walks around the neighborhood and learned about the different trees and their leaves; we picked up acorns and learned about how they grow into trees; and we noticed the many different shapes of rocks.

The activity I enjoyed the most, though, was what I called circle time. We sat in a circle; and as we went around the circle, I said something like this to each child, "You have such a pretty smile. It lights up the whole room! Tell us something you like about yourself." At first, it was hard for the children to think of anything to say, but when they got the hang of it, they loved the activity and they begged to do it. Their responses ranged from, "I like my hair" to "I like it when I help my teacher."

Holidays were fun with the children. At Halloween we carved a jack-o-lantern. We enjoyed its smiling, toothy face; then laughed to return on a Monday morning and find a shriveled-face pumpkin. At Thanksgiving, we let the children make Pilgrim and Indian costumes, and all the teachers went in together to prepare a huge Thanksgiving meal, complete with turkey and dressing, sweet potato casserole, and all the trimmings. At Christmas I bought a live tree for my classroom, and the children made decorations by looping together strips of paper to make a chain.

Just as I had high expectations of myself, I also had high expectations of my students. They worked hard and were proud of their accomplishments. We had a store in our classroom, and the students earned real money for doing good work. Their store was stocked with items of different value, from five cents all the way to five dollars. Students who needed immediate gratification could use their five cents to buy a brightly colored pencil, a small pad of sticky notes, or a sticker with a funny face on it. Other students, with an eye toward bigger prizes, decided to save their money and buy a game, a small flashlight, a funny calendar, or a photograph album.

Every teacher has a collection of never-to-be-forgotten incidents. Here are a few that still make me smile. One Christmas we took the students to a nursing home to sing carols. As we were leaving, one elderly lady said pleasantly, "You all come back now," to which my dear little Eddie replied, "Don't count on it!" One afternoon Sylvester asked if they could go outside. I replied, "We'll go out in a little while but not right now." That wasn't the answer Sylvester wanted to hear, so he asked another teacher. She responded, "Now what did Miss Maxine say?" Sylvester repeated my answer precisely, perfectly imitating my speech! Everybody broke into laughter.

Little Red was my life for six years. I loved it so much that I would do anything not to miss one single day. During that time, though, I decided I wanted to pursue an advanced degree. In the meantime, I had become interested in computer programming, and I couldn't decide whether to stay in education or change to a business focus. I will never forget the day I went to talk with Fred about my dilemma. He thought for a minute and then said something that changed my life forever. He said, "You're a damned good teacher." That was all I needed to hear. I knew that education, in some form, would remain my career – my life's calling.

The Long Road to the Doctorate

Returning to my undergraduate alma mater, Delta State University, I sat in the office of the Dean and told him that I would like to enter the doctoral program in education. He said something that stunned me. "This program is not for you. I can't guarantee that you would get a job with this degree." My heart sank. Was he denying me admission? I met all the criteria. I had a Master's degree with a 4.0 GPA, I had taught for four years, and I had three outstanding letters of recommendation. However, none of those things made me any more able to walk, use my hands, or speak fluently. I supposed those were the criteria that I was lacking, and those were the criteria that I would never have.

Back at home, I went to see a close friend, one with red hair that suited her personality to a tee. Pam never minced any words. "That's illegal!" she said with ferociousness. "He can't do that. You meet all the requirements. Just write him a letter, and then go sign up for classes." She made it sound so simple.

I did exactly what Pam suggested. I wrote the Dean a letter and told him that I met all the criteria for admission to the doctoral program and that I wanted in! Then, when it was time to register for classes, I boldly wheeled up to the counter where the Dean was signing off on students' class schedules. I handed him my schedule for the first round of doctoral level courses. I smiled; he smiled and signed it, and I moved on with a giggle of triumph. One more hurdle down!

For the next two years, I taught school and took classes at night and during the summers. My schedule was horrendous. Many days I taught all day at Little Red, then drove 45 miles to class, stayed until 9 o'clock, then caught a ride home. My weekends were spent doing homework.

Even though the classes were hard, I liked to think that they were challenging. Somehow, it's more fun to do well in a difficult class than to do well in an easy one. One of my professors, Dr. Starr, took delight in giving those who passed his course a pencil with the words "I Survived Starr" written on it.

My doctoral program was small, so those of us who were in it became very close. That's one of the things I enjoyed most about it. The friendships I formed with Tom, Jack, and Evelyn became lifetime friendships. Tom completed his degree before I did, and he began working for the Continuing Studies program at the college. His office was on my way to class, and many days he would invite me in to chat. His encouragement always lifted my spirits.

My parents were my hands and feet during this time, as always. They spent hours in the library making copies of articles for me. For about three months, I slept only four hours a night while I completed my dissertation. My topic dealt with the types of diplomas that students with learning disabilities received. I mailed surveys to every high school in the state and waited anxiously every day for the mail to come to see what my response rate was. If I didn't get enough responses, my research wouldn't be valid. After three rounds of mailings, I finally had enough completed surveys to finish my dissertation.

To complicate matters, this was the time when computers were in their infancy and high quality printers were too expensive for the ordinary person. My dissertation had to be typed, and the individual who normally typed dissertations was unavailable, so my mother assumed that task and did an incredible job.

In April 1987, I "defended" my dissertation – a process that's like being grilled by several committee members over an open flame. I was required to answer questions from the committee to support my study, after which the committee would decide whether the work I had done was worthy of my being awarded a doctorate degree. Actually, my grilling wasn't as bad as I had anticipated, but I felt a lot of pressure knowing that my degree hinged on this "defense." After my committee had finished questioning me, they asked me to leave the room while they made their decision. When they called me back into the room, the committee chairman shook my hand and said, "Congratulations, Dr. Harper!" I breathed a huge sigh of relief.

As I left the building that afternoon, a cloud dumped a bucketful of rain on me. Soaking wet, I rode the 45 miles home as happy as could be. Wanda was evidently quite confident of my success because she was waiting at home for me with a celebration dinner of fried chicken, one of my favorite meals.

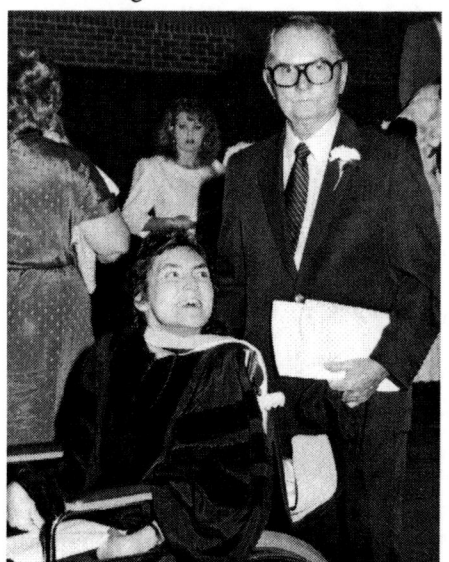

The day of graduation is still vivid in my memory. Our friends Homer and Ouida came, and Ouida helped me pin my cap to my hair. Then, as I sat on the stage and waited for the ceremony to begin, I looked around for Wanda and saw her walking around the balcony. I loved catching a glimpse of her and realizing that she was wearing my favorite of all her maternity dresses – the pink one with

49

tiny flowers.

Finally it was time for the big moment – my hooding. The Dean who initially had reservations about letting me into the program had become my biggest fan, and he was the one who placed that treasured hood around my neck. Then the entire audience broke into applause, followed by a standing ovation! After graduation, I was pleasantly surprised by the people who had come to share my success. My high school principal came and gave me a sincere hug of congratulations. Later that afternoon, my parents had a graduation party for me and invited all of my relatives. It was a perfect ending to a very long road.

The Cottonseed Queen and Her Gentle Knights

I had finished my Doctorate, and the big job search was on. Fortunately, I didn't have to look far. A friend offered me the opportunity of going into business with him to develop software for school districts.

I enjoyed learning how to write computer programs and make them do my bidding. The work was long and tedious but fun and interesting at the same time. We programmed in DOS, and my first PC had a 20 megabyte hard drive. I thought that would hold all the data in the world. Little did I know how quickly technology would change!

After the software was developed, sales were good. I made many friends as I traveled to schools throughout Texas and Mississippi. I still laugh as I remember being in the computer room at one of the schools when a teacher walked into the outer office, peeked in at me and said, "I thought the computer guy was coming."

I looked up at her and said, "I am the computer guy."

With a puzzled look, she said, "You don't look like a computer guy."

"I'm glad of that," I smiled.

As I became more proficient in programming, our company began to attract clients in the business world. We became specialists in designing software for cottonseed gins. One day there was a meeting with a company that had an inaccessible building. One of the guys remarked, "I think we should have the meeting at your place so Maxine can be there." My involvement with the cottonseed industry earned me the nickname "Cottonseed Queen."

I also did programming for the public library. It was fun knowing that my handiwork was behind the scenes every time someone checked out a book.

More important to me than the work I was doing, though, were the people I met during those nine years. They were my gentle knights, teaching me life lessons that one doesn't expect to encounter in a sterile computer environment.

I developed software for the Escambia County School District in Pensacola, Florida. There I met Malcolm, who was in charge of the assessment reporting for children in special education. He asked me to design a particular program that would take student information from the main system and let teachers put it into their individualized education programs for students. I'll never forget the day when I first demonstrated the program live to him. He got this gigantic grin on his face and said, "Wow! I've been waiting my whole career to see this!" Talk about a boost to my ego – that was it!

Another of my experiences in Florida was that of attending a conference where we demonstrated our software. To be quite honest, the conference was a total bore – until I met Marilyn. She walked up to my booth and said, "You have cerebral palsy, don't you?" I smiled and said, "Yes, I do." This opened the door to a conversation that I will never forget.

Marilyn proceeded to tell me that she had a little boy with cerebral palsy – a very severe form, and he was not expected to live very long. In an emotion-packed voice, she told me all about him – about how she held him in her lap for hours at a time, how she fought against his having a feeding tube and succeeded in getting him to eat on his own, and how she was so afraid to leave him even for a moment. The thing I remember most, though, is her description of how she rigged up his chair so he could go trick-or-treating. "I attached a tape recorder to his chair and recorded the phrase, 'Trick-or-Treat!' Then I concocted a device that would allow him to activate the recorder with his elbow. He nailed it!" The look on her face with that last statement told me that she took such great delight in the smallest accomplishments in her little boy's young life. Events such as this reveal to me that God brings strangers together for brief moments in time to build us up and let us know that we are not alone in our plight.

Another person who stands out in my memory during that time in my life is a young man named Shane, who came to work for us when he was in high school. I remember Shane as a brown-haired (Beatles style) young man whose favorite article of clothing was a tie-dyed tee shirt with rainbow colors. He was as close to a genius as anyone I had ever met. Shane knew computers like the back of his hand, and he learned to program with the ease of a Mozart learning to write music. I had the unique opportunity of teaching Shane to use a special programming technique called Btrieve, which he caught on to like a whiz. He was as thrilled as though I had taught him to slalom.

Although most teenagers who were as brilliant as Shane might have been cocky, Shane was anything but cocky. He was a down-to-earth, solid, all-around great guy.

One evening when Shane and I were the only ones left at the office, I received a tech support call from someone wanting to know how to install our software. "What do you type when you put the first disk in?" she asked. I was trying to tell her to type "setup." Somehow the message wasn't getting through. The caller was having a difficult time understanding my speech. From across the hall, Shane could hear that I was in distress. He came to my rescue and told the caller what I was saying. When he hung up the phone for me, he grinned and said, "Some people just can't understand plain English." I knew he said that to make me feel better about my less than perfect speech.

I wish I could tell you that the Shane story had a happy ending, that he went on to a distinguished college and fulfilled his desire for a career with Microsoft. Shane did go on to college, and he continued to work for us. Then, on the day after his twenty-first birthday, I received a call from one of the owners of the computer firm where we worked. The voice said shakily, "Shane had an accident last night, and he didn't make it." The car in which he was riding was hit head on. Shane was in the back seat with the seatbelt across his waist. In characteristic Shane fashion, he had taken care to repair the seatbelt for the front passenger side of the car, thereby saving the life of that young lady. Immediately after the accident, Shane was able to get out of the automobile, but he had sustained massive internal injuries. He was taken to a trauma center where he died from blood loss. His funeral was one of the most difficult I have ever attended. At the end, everyone released a white balloon into the air. I like to think that Shane's spirit became as free as those white balloons, but the world will be a little less without Shane in it.

Nine years is a significant span in one's life, and those nine years of my life were enriched beyond measure by the people I met along the way and whose memory will follow me the rest of my days.

Our House

I wheeled down the ramp of my van and gazed longingly at the vacant, overgrown lot next to my parents' house. I desperately wanted that small plot of land. I wanted to build a home of my own right there. But there was one problem. The gentleman who owned the property didn't want to sell it. I had asked him twice already, and each time he had said "No, I think my daughter and I want to hold onto it."

I was confused. I really thought the Lord wanted me to have my own home – to have the freedom to go in and out as I wanted, to see the moon and stars at night, to have friends over any time I wanted without disturbing my parents. There was something about living in a home of my own that would give me an identity, a sense of as much independence as was possible for me.

I had already pored over house plans and selected one I liked and could adapt to meet my needs. The house was beautiful, with a stately roof and long, arched windows across the front. But the door to my house wouldn't open.

As I looked over at that vacant lot, I heard the words, "Ask and it shall be given you." (Matthew 7:7)

"But dear Lord, I've already asked twice. How can I ask again?"

"Just trust me and ask."

And so I asked a third time. The response was, "Let me call my daughter and get back with you."

Oh, how I hated the thought of waiting, only to be turned down again. But this time the reply was different. "We've decided to sell you the lot." Oh, the joy that raced through my heart!

Now came the task of selecting a contractor. I got bids from three men. After talking with one of them, I decided that he didn't listen carefully enough to what I wanted. Another wanted up front money, which scared me away. The third impressed me by his desire to do everything just like I wanted. When I called to talk with him one Wednesday evening, I got his answering machine and asked him to call me back. "I was at prayer meeting," he explained when he returned my call. I smiled and said, "You've got the job."

Tony became tied up on another job, and it was four months later, the first Saturday in March 1994, when the foundation of my house was laid. Tony was there, carefully guiding the process. So much depended on the foundation. It had to be sloped just right in order for my roll-in shower to drain properly. As I watched the concrete being poured, I was humbled, yet very much at peace about this awesome project I was beginning. The words rang loud and clear through my heart and mind: "Except the Lord build the house, they labor in vain that build it." (Psalm 127:1) This house must be built to the glory of God.

The next four months were a flurry of activity as the house went up. My mother and I, and often my aunt Laura Lee, rode through neighborhoods looking for a house with brick to my liking. Nothing was exactly what I wanted. "I'll know it when I see it," I said. So we kept riding and looking. Finally, we came to a relatively new house that had a beautiful, pinkish color brick with gray specks. "That's it!" I screamed. But what was the name of that brick? "We'll certainly find out," said my mother (who was ready to stop driving around). Fortunately, the owners of the house were standing in the front yard. We stopped and inquired about the brick. "It's called Canterbury," the lady said. "It's a new brick. In fact, this house was the first to be built with this brick." So Canterbury it was.

To my parents' credit, I was able to select everything to suit my own taste. Mama drove me around to look at roofs, mortar, and paint colors. Daddy hauled wallpaper books by the armload.

Even before the house had a foundation, it had a stained glass window. I found the window at a shop called The Glass Rainbow, whose owner had taken the glass from a 100-year-old church that was being demolished. He recrafted the glass into a window, in the center of which is a large cross of deep crimson that changes color with the sun's position. Surrounding the cross is a type of yellow cathedral glass that gives the window a special glow. The house was built around that window!

Of course, I was careful to get the special features I needed in the house, like low light switches, an automatic door, lever handles, bathroom sinks with space for me to wheel up under them, grab bars in the bathroom and bedroom, and a roll-in shower. The room that was supposed to be the dining room became my office, and the breakfast room became the dining area. The entire living area is open, with no doors except into the bedrooms and bathrooms. The openness makes the house seem larger than it actually is.

What makes the house really special to me, though, is the blessing I prayed upon it. One Saturday, soon after the interior walls had gone up and I could actually see the individual rooms, I went over to the house and stayed there alone for several hours. I wheeled from one room to the next; and at each room I stopped and prayed that God would bless that room.

In the living room I prayed, "May all who enter this home feel your love and your peace surrounding them. I may not always know their needs; but you, oh God, know the needs of all your children. Please meet my family and my friends where they are, and let them feel your presence here in this home."

In the kitchen I prayed, "May we recognize you as the Bread of Life and the Living Water; and may we, in this home, look to you to satisfy our spiritual hunger and thirst. May we, your children, fellowship around the table in this room, feeling free to share our joys and our sorrows with each other. And may the food we eat here strengthen us to serve you faithfully."

In my office I prayed, "May the work that I do here glorify you and bring you honor. Bless my labor, that it may produce the fruits you desire."

In the guest rooms I prayed, "May those who rest here find true rest in you. Please lighten their burden and ease their loneliness as they come to you for comfort and strength. May they be quiet in this room, quiet enough to hear your still, small voice."

In my own bedroom I prayed, "Lord, you know how needy I am – how weak, how helpless. I ask you to live here with me, be my friend, my helper, my constant source of strength. Please take away all fear and replace it with total, unwavering trust in you."

Through the years God truly has blessed this house. One day my cousin Lisa was walking through the house, and she remarked, "This sure is a happy house." In his goodness, God has brought to our house the fellowship of family and friends; he has allowed me to feel his presence here; and he has given me the assurance that he will never leave me nor forsake me. For I am his, and he is mine.

Out of the Mouths of Babes

Children have an uncanny way of speaking the truth without hesitation. One afternoon during my college days, I was sitting in the lobby of Ward Hall waiting to see my professor. It just so happened that my professor's 9-year-old daughter was also there waiting for her mother. The youngster walked up to me and, with a wise, all-knowing look, said, "Do you know you're handicapped?" Actually, the thought had crossed my mind a time or two, but I guess I needed a child to confirm my suspicions.

On another occasion, my mother and I were shopping for a wedding gift when a little boy felt the need to enlighten me about speaking properly. To the store owner's dismay, her three-year-old grandson happened to be wandering around in the store while we were there. The little fellow wasn't shy in the least. Hearing me talk, he walked up to me, put a finger to my lips, and said, "Now you talk right." I explained to him that this was just the way I had to talk. "No," he said, "you talk right!" By this time the grandmother had turned a hundred shades of red. She suggested that perhaps he needed to go to the restroom, to which he replied, "No, I don't. She just needs to talk right."

The conversation between my cousin and her little boy went something like this:
"You said Maxine is really smart?" asked the little boy.
"She sure is!" replied his mother.
"Then how come she hasn't figured out how to walk yet?"

My cousin and her family were visiting one weekend when her young daughter began to wonder why I wasn't getting any better. Surely someone could help me.
"Can the policeman help you?"
"No, honey, I'm afraid not."
"What about the fireman?"
"No, he can't help either."
We were running out of community helpers, so I said, "There's really no one who can help me."
"No one except God?"

Out of the mouths of babes.

Aunt Elma

The cars stopped along the roadside as the queen passed by. But the roadside wasn't the English countryside, nor was the queen's name Elizabeth. The road was a winding country road in the hills of Carroll County, Mississippi, and the queen was my Aunt Elma. The cars were waiting in reverence as her funeral procession made its way to the family cemetery.

I wish everyone in those cars could have known Aunt Elma. She was royalty to all who did know her. She put everyone before herself. But it was the little things that added up to the big things.

Her house was my favorite place to go. It was the gathering place – everyone's second home. I don't remember ever hearing a knock at her door. Everyone just went in because it was home. You opened the door, and the smell of homemade rolls greeted you, followed by a hug. Aunt Elma was always scurrying around, making sure everyone had found a place to sit, had gotten a glass of iced tea, or had sniffed their way to the cocoons covered with powdered sugar. I loved spending entire afternoons sitting around the big table in her kitchen, with everybody talking and laughing as a light breeze fluttered through the open window.

Holidays were, of course, spent at Aunt Elma's house. Thanksgiving began with a colorful drive through the countryside and continued with a banquet that filled the kitchen and flowed over into the living room. In the afternoon we cousins enjoyed walking to the creek and playing games of touch football. I was always part of the fun, even if it meant handing me over the fence from one cousin to another. "Here, you take her, then I'll pass the chair over." Being part of the extended family of which Aunt Elma was the matriarch provided me with happy traditions that reinforced my identity as a valued family member.

When I was young, Aunt Elma was my Sunday School teacher. I remember feeling so loved by her. On the Sunday I proudly told her that I had been accepted into "regular" school, the joy on her face was as tangible as the tight hug she gave me. She followed my achievements with delight and always shared my happiness as though I were her own daughter. Her wisdom became apparent to me when, during my senior year in high school, I was pronounced valedictorian. At that time Aunt Elma worked as a proofreader for the local newspaper. As is common with the media, the newspaper wanted to "play up" my disability in the article announcing my accomplishment. Fortunately, the reporter asked the advice of my aunt. Wisely, she persuaded the newspaper to let me enjoy this special time in my life as a normal teenager, with no mention of my disability. I remember reading that article with such pride, thinking, "I'm not different after all."

Time passed, and adulthood arrived. As my age increased, so did my closeness with Aunt Elma. When Wanda became pregnant, I could hardly wait for her to share the news with Aunt Elma, whose face glowed with joy and anticipation. And oh, what a thrill it was to take two-week-old Avent to meet her great aunt! Aunt Elma gently cupped Avent's head in her hands as she gazed at her with the awe and wonder of someone who understands the miracle of life and knows the One who is the source of life.

As Avent grew, Aunt Elma took delight in her funny nature and quick wit. One Christmas when Avent was about two years old, we had gathered at Aunt Elma's house as usual. Fascinated by the icicles on the Christmas tree, Avent began taking off one after another even as Wanda begged her to leave the pretty icicles on the tree. Finally, caught with an icicle in her hands and Wanda asking, "What are you doing?" Avent replied, "I'm flossing my teeth." Aunt Elma broke out into her own soft but hearty laughter.

Aunt Elma lived 80 wonderful years. Leukemia slowly, stealthily stole her stamina; then it stole her life. I wasn't ready for her to go. I still had stories to share with her about Avent; I still wanted to be able to call every night and hear her voice at the other end. She spent her last week in the hospital. The morphine kept her asleep most of the time, except when the pain broke through and her eyes fluttered and her lips quivered. It was then I knew that I had to let her go. The queen had to go home to the palace waiting for her in heaven.

The Valley Church

It was the last night of revival services at our small church, and I noticed that all the men were gathered around Charles' car. They were digging deep into their pockets and handing over to Charles whatever they could. I surmised that our collections during the week hadn't been enough to pay the minister. Finally I saw Charles counting the money one last time. Then he smiled, and there proceeded to be a lot of handshaking. I gathered that we had met our goal.

Ours was by no means a miserly congregation. It was a small congregation with lots of elderly members on fixed incomes, plus a number of households with only one wage earner. No matter – whatever we lacked in dollar bills, we made up for in hugs.

When I came home at age 8 from that long brick building two hours away, my family was at last freed from years of making the 200-mile round trek to see me every Sunday. We could now go to church. Daddy wanted to go back to his Carroll County roots, to the church where his elder brother, my Uncle Moss, was pastor.

It was a 17-mile drive to church, but every Sunday was like a combination worship service and family reunion. We had all the quaint idiosyncrasies of a country church. We all waited patiently while the older folks tested their hearing devices ("Aunt Connie, can you hear?"). We also waited patiently while one of the great aunts made change from the collection plate. And no one minded that another great aunt sang off key – very loudly. It was the sweetness that counted.

Aunt Elma taught the children's Sunday School class. Oh, how I loved her! We learned all the familiar Bible stories; and we learned, too, the love of God from her own love for us. I remember the Sunday I told Aunt Elma that I was going to be allowed to go to regular school with my sister Wanda and our cousin Lisa. She smiled with surprise and squeezed me tightly to her.

In my own life, being a Christian didn't spring from any sudden, dramatic conversion. It was as though I had been born believing. Still, I wanted to publicly profess my faith and be baptized. So when I was 9 years old, during a revival service, I went forward and took my stand as a believer and follower of Jesus Christ. Since our church had no baptismal font, a few weeks later we all went to Aunt Lottie's pond for my baptism. With Daddy supporting me on one side and Uncle Moss on the other, I waded into the water, and Uncle Moss baptized me into the family of God. I remember so distinctly the sight of my empty wheelchair parked on the bank of the pond. Why is that memory so clear? Years later, when Avent was a young child, she asked me one day, "Mackie, are there wheelie chairs in heaven?"

"No, Peanut," I replied. "No one will need them there."

God allowed me to be baptized without my wheelchair. "Oh, what a foretaste of glory divine!"

I loved our church's traditions – the "dinners on the ground," the Christmas pageants, the Easter egg hunts, the summer revival services. I'll always remember our potluck dinners with Aunt Elma's sweet creamed corn, Linda's onion smothered squash, Laura Lee's ham balls, and Aunt Molly's caramel pie. Come to think of it, they weren't potluck dinners at all; they were banquets fit for a king. The Christmas pageants were always fun, with makeshift scenery and little voices whispering, "People are coming in" and "I already said my line." Fun, too, were the egg hunts in the grassy field around the church. Youngsters barely old enough to walk held an adult hand and, wide-eyed at finding a brightly colored egg, stooped to pick it up and put it in their basket. Every summer, our church's revival brought longtime friends from Fort Worth to bless us with a week of hymns and sermons.

In my adulthood Uncle Macey taught our Sunday School class. He was an ardent admirer of the Apostle Paul, and he led us in studies of Paul's teachings on his missionary journeys. Uncle Macey liked Paul's personality and would have been pleased that his last grandchild was named Paul Macey. When quoting the Apostle Paul, Uncle Macey would often laugh, particularly at statements like "Therefore if thine enemy hunger, feed him; if he thirst, give him drink: for in so doing thou shalt heap coals of fire on his head." (Romans 12:20, KJV) Uncle Macey's motto, though, was Micah 6:8, "What doth the Lord require of thee, but to do justice, to love mercy, and to walk humbly with thy God."

Uncle Moss was perhaps the most humble minister I've ever met. He stood quietly in the pulpit and spoke to us, more like a teacher than a preacher. He seemed never to feel quite worthy of the pulpit. One Sunday he confessed that he didn't feel adequately prepared to preach that day, whereupon his precious wife Violet suggested, "Well, sit down then." We were glad he didn't mind her that time.

In his gentle manner, Uncle Moss often used stories in his sermons to teach us unforgettable lessons. Calling on us to be peacemakers, he told the story of two elderly women with a longstanding grudge against each other. The grudge melted away when a mutual friend, a peacemaker, told one of the women about a compliment that the other had paid her.

To illustrate the difference kindness can make, Uncle Moss told the story of a man who dreamed that he went to the gates of hell and peered in. There was a long banquet table filled with delicious foods. But the people sitting around the table were hungry and disgruntled because they had long metal extenders on their arms, making it impossible for them to feed themselves. The man then dreamed that he went to the gates of heaven and peered in. At first everything looked the same. There was the same long banquet table filled with delicious foods. Even here the people had metal extenders on their arms that prevented them from feeding themselves. Yet no one here was hungry; in fact, everyone was smiling and happy. They were reaching out in love to feed one another.

In another sermon about our inborn inclination to believe in Someone greater than ourselves, Uncle Moss told the story of the atheist who, at the deathbed of his beloved daughter, said, "I would not have you die in my unbelief, but in your mother's living Christ."

As time went by at the Valley, I began to teach Sunday School for Uncle Macey when he was away. I wrote the lessons so I could express myself better. Later, when Uncle Macey asked me to be the full time teacher, I threw myself into the task wholeheartedly. I read, studied, prayed, and wrote – wrote in the same way as always, one precious keystroke at a time. And every Sunday, as I heard those I loved reading the words I had written, my heart overflowed with joy. Looking back, this time of writing was one of the happiest and most fulfilling periods of my life.

The time came when Uncle Moss decided to retire from preaching. We were blessed to be able to get students from Reformed Theological Seminary to fill our pulpit. They were scholarly men, highly knowledgeable in the word of the Lord. We enjoyed the friendships we formed with them and their families. Steve and Karen were the first young couple, very sweet and easy to get to know. They were followed by Tom and Sue, with their five children. What fun we had being with them! I loved the sight of their green van pulling up and all the kids piling out. Tom and Sue stayed with us for about three years, and we became very close to them. The last family to stay with us for a long time was Dennis and Mary and their son Drew. We grew close to them as well, and Dennis preached two funerals for us and officiated at the wedding of Michael, one of our family members.

In 1998 we decided to try to raise the funds to build onto the church an annex – an entryway with, of all things, a restroom. Our church had never had a restroom; we had always "borrowed" restrooms in the homes of members who lived nearby. Due to the generosity of current members, as well as those who had grown up in the church and wanted to see it continue, the annex was built.

It was dedicated on Easter Sunday 1999.

These words were spoken in tribute to the church: "There has never been anything big about the Valley Church – except its faith and its heart. But these two gifts have touched lives too numerous to count. Those who come through its doors remember it forever. They find here the secret of life, peace, and joy – a personal knowledge of our Lord and Savior, Jesus Christ. They find, too, that they have value both in the eyes of God and in the eyes of His people. There is a love here that, once experienced, is never forgotten."

Daffodils in the Snow

It was another of those late Saturday nights when I was finishing writing my Sunday School lesson for the next day. I had learned that my lessons were being passed around for others to read, and I felt honored.

When I had accumulated a good sized collection of lessons, my Aunt Elma encouraged me to put the lessons into book form. For a time I resisted, thinking that my writings were not worthy of that distinction. But finally the book began to unfold as I sequenced the lessons according to the Christian calendar, just as I had done when I taught them. There was a lesson to bring in the New Year; there were lessons for Easter, for Mother's Day and Father's Day; there were lessons for Thanksgiving; and there were four lessons for the four Sundays of Advent. For the summer months I wrote lessons that centered on the Fruits of the Spirit. I think my favorite series, though, explored each verse of the Twenty-Third Psalm from the viewpoint of a sheep and its relationship with its shepherd. Especially dear to me was the Introduction, in which I wrote about the little family church that inspired my writing.

The title of the book, "Daffodils in the Snow," came from my love of daffodils, which are the flower of hope, the first flower of spring. I love the image of tiny yellow heads of daffodils peeking out from banks of soft, white snow.

In the book's preface, I wrote:

Life taught me early on that seasons of wintry sorrow, pain, disappointment, and even grief are part of the human condition. Yet God somehow penetrates the drifts of snow with the promise of spring. Through His daffodils in the snow, He makes us know that He is in control of all things and that there is no sadness or adversity that His love, joy, and purity cannot shine through and overcome. He is uniquely able to take the frozen hillsides of our hearts and lives, melt them with His warm, abiding presence, and transform them into fields of blooming flowers that turn their faces up to Him.

May this book bring you many daffodils of hope as you discover for yourself the presence and the power of the living God in your own life.

The process of writing and self-publishing my book was something I enjoyed more than I could have ever imagined. I knew the chances were slim that a publishing company would receive my book enthusiastically, at least not in the form that I wanted it (with descriptions of my little country church and its members like Uncle Buddy), so I decided to establish my own publishing company and have the book printed myself. I chose the name "Lantern Publishing Company" after the scripture that says "The light shines in the darkness, and the darkness did not overcome it" (John 1:5, New Revised Standard Version).

With the title of the book firmly decided, the search was on to find just the right picture for the cover. I found several stock photography companies and asked them to send me pictures conveying the image of daffodils in snow. I received everything from one tiny wilted daffodil in a huge bank of snow to a whole field of daffodils with no snow. I really wanted perky daffodils in a country setting with just the right amount of snow. Okay, I was being really picky. But finally a stock photographer sent me a picture of about a half dozen beautiful yellow daffodils sprouting up from a layer of cottony white snow in a country setting. Just exactly what I wanted!

Wanda designed the cover and did the layout for the book, and we found a printing company that would work with us on making copies of the book. In October 1995, two thousand copies of Daffodils in the Snow arrived at our house. Our front porch became a book warehouse, and my mother became a book seller. Our local newspaper published an article about the book in November, with a picture of Avent and me, with Avent holding the book in her hands. The first weekend in December, our local craft show was held at the Civic Center, and I took my book as my "ware." On Saturday, I sold 100 signed copies, and on Sunday I sold another 30 copies. Needless to say, I was ecstatic.

The book continued to do well, especially since I didn't do any real marketing. I did do a book signing at That Bookstore in Blytheville, Arkansas, where my friend Patsy lived. The book store had studio chairs that their guest authors signed. I felt giddy signing the same studio chair that John Grisham had signed. What I enjoyed most, though, were the comments that came from persons who read the book or who gave it as a gift. One story from Patsy especially touched my heart. She wrote:

"I had given my friend a copy during her battle with breast cancer. She lost that battle but taught us all so very much about love and courage. Her husband John called me about 8 months after her death and said he finally went through her night stand and opened her favorite book...Daffodils! She had marked your chapter on love and John said it was as though his wife sent that as a gift from heaven to him. He said he took your book out on the patio every morning with a cup of coffee and "nourished" his hurting heart with Daffodils."

Special Solutions

My new office space was a dream. It wasn't elaborate by any means. In fact, it was old and almost rustic, but it had character – high ceilings, large rooms, and a picture window that looked out onto the distinguished courthouse across the street.

Yes, I was taking yet another leap – establishing my own business. Even though I knew it would begin as a computer software development business, I had the freedom to let it evolve into whatever form was right for it – and for me. Thus, its original name – Software Solutions – the name under which I opened it in March 1997 – later changed to Special Solutions.

I was meticulous about the equipment I purchased for my new company. Determined to buy the best computers for the lowest price, I pored over magazines and devoured articles comparing different brands of computers, printers, and storage media. Zip drives were the newest portable storage devices. I bought one for work and one for home so I could continue my common practice of bringing work home.

My detailed, high-expectations advertisement for an administrative assistant elicited my mother's comment, "You'll never find anyone who can do all that." But Debbe answered my ad, and she was exactly what I needed to help me get my business off the ground. By the end of the very first day, she had arranged the furniture in both of our offices, unpacked and assembled two computers and printers, gotten two phone lines installed, and helped me respond to my first request for a "software solution."

My company served a wide variety of clients, including a helicopter company that sprayed acres of land with chemicals for different purposes, a chain of convenience stores, and a business that sold the meal and hulls from cotton and soybeans. Obviously, I served a clientele in a rural area. My clients were kind, down-home folks.

In addition to serving clients locally, I developed customized software for educational diagnosticians – those specialists who give intelligence and achievement tests to children who may need special education services. The need was great in Texas, where the regulations were most stringent, so that's where I focused my efforts.

It was about two years later that I found myself sitting in a room filled with about 30 educational diagnosticians in Arlington, Texas. They were there to hear my sales pitch for the software I had written – software that took test scores and interpreted their meaning, making the diagnosticians' report writing easier.

What a contrast there was between me and my competitor's sales representative! I never met him, but I saw him and I felt pretty intimidated. With his dark suit, briefcase, brisk walk, firm handshake, and easy conversation style, he fit the part of a salesperson to a tee. I, on the other hand, sat in my wheelchair, held my fisted hand out shakily, and spoke with eagerness but not ease. Nothing about me conjured up the image of a salesperson.

I really wanted – needed – this contract. But what could I say or do that would give me enough credibility to land the sale? I prayed for guidance. Admittedly, it was one of those quick "Help me" prayers, but I needed quick help.

Then I did something I hadn't planned to do. I began by saying, "I'm not a salesperson. I guess that's pretty obvious. I'm just someone who cares about kids – someone who cares that they get the services they need and that people like you have the tools you need to serve them well." I went on to tell the story of my own rocky start as a child trying to enter the world of education. As I spoke, I looked around the room and saw smiling faces and a few eyes brimming with tears. In just a few brief moments, these strangers had become my friends. Sure, I still hoped to get the sale (and I did get it), but even more important to me, I related both to my audience's human side and to their professional side. We connected!

Fortunately for me, Judy was assigned to be my liaison with the school district. Judy was very detail-oriented, which was great because developing software requires the highest attention to detail. Over the next months, Judy and I became close friends. She spent numerous weekends working with me at my house as she made the astute observation that she could hide out here and no one would find her. When we were apart, we e-mailed regularly, usually around midnight since we were both night owls. One night after a particularly rough day, I e-mailed Judy and said, "You know a cat has nine lives? Well, I just killed another cat."

My original plan was that my company would evolve into more than just a software business. And that's exactly what happened. I began to do a variety of other work – usually computer related but very expansive.

A dear friend, Kathleen (whom you'll hear more about later), had gone to work for the University of Mississippi (Ole Miss) and had been named director of a research and evaluation center there. I began working with Kathleen on some projects for her center, and I found that I enjoyed the type of work her center was doing. To my delight, I found that through my company, God was opening doors for me that I would have never dreamed possible.

Another Career Change

It was late afternoon on Thursday, June 15, 2000. I had just returned to my Special Solutions office after a day of consulting work at Ole Miss. The phone was ringing; and when I answered, a voice at the other end said, "May I speak with Maxine Harper?"

After ascertaining that I was the party she wanted, the voice said, "I'm calling from the Human Resources office at the University of Mississippi. We would like to offer you the position of Educational Research Analyst for the Center for Educational Research and Evaluation. Will you accept the position?"

This was the call I had been waiting for. I tried to keep my composure as I replied, "I'll be happy to accept the position." I had applied weeks before, as soon as the job was advertised. Oh, how I wanted it – how I needed it! Work that I loved under the direction of a friend I'd known for 20 years! What's more, I would finally have the health benefits that had eluded me for years. What more could I ask for!

I began work on Monday, June 19, 2000. My first office was in the old School of Education building – the building that was once University High School. Office space was at a premium, especially downstairs, where my office had to be located because there was no elevator. So … my first office had actually once been a book closet! And it was separated from Kathleen's office by stairs – lots of stairs.

I loved my job. And the people I worked with accepted me warmly and graciously. Mr. Akey, the network administrator, had an office near mine. He was always ready with a kind word and a helping hand. In fact, he came to my rescue so often that I began to call him my guardian angel.

My first task was to develop an evaluation plan for the Barksdale Reading Institute. To learn more about the program, I attended the institute's orientation for its reading coordinators. The coordinators were kind, intelligent ladies with a passion for teaching reading. They were easy to get to know and fun to be with. Meeting them and learning about their program proved to be the perfect way to begin my new job.

Also special to me beyond words were the many student workers whose hands and feet made me productive and whose voices filled my office with the joy and vibrancy of youth. In addition to office work like typing, filing, and answering the phone, my student workers often helped me eat lunch. In fact, Audrey sometimes brought me lunch from the sorority house and fed it to me. The students seemed to enjoy helping me and to thrive from their closeness with me.

One day Kathleen remarked, "I don't know what you do to these students, but somehow they're changed from being around you." I had no explanation other than perhaps they were unaccustomed to having anyone in a higher position allow them to enter her life as closely as I allowed them to enter mine. And maybe – just maybe – they sensed that I liked them, that I loved them.

A Second Home

When I went to work at Ole Miss, the most difficult aspect was that it was 90 miles from my house! For the first few months, Ruthie, my friend and helper, drove me to Ole Miss several days a week and I worked from home the other days. As time went by, though, I decided to look for a house in Oxford where I could live during the week.

On Labor Day, Mama, Daddy and I went house hunting. The realtor warned, "I don't really know if I have any houses that would meet your needs. In fact, I know of only one house that might be a possibility. Let's go take a look."

We drove up to a fairly ordinary looking brick house in a modest neighborhood. We went in through the garage; and since there was only one step into the back door, Daddy was able to use some plywood boards to build a makeshift ramp.

The garage door opened into a combination living room/dining room. The living room had a beautiful cathedral ceiling, and the dining room had an archway that opened into a modern looking kitchen with lots of cabinet space and a small pantry. Down the hall from the living room, there were three spacious bedrooms, one of which had been turned into an office.

The house was decorated beautifully, and I immediately fell in love with it. I liked its openness, its large rooms. Then I noticed something incredible – the light switches were low! Even more incredible, there was a 12-by-20-foot exercise room just off the dining room. Perhaps a roll-in shower could be built there! Sure enough, the realtor called a contractor who came right over and said, "Oh, that won't be a problem." I felt that house was meant to be mine!

But the miracles had only begun. In the master bedroom, I noticed that the bed was unusually low, just as I needed it. So I asked the realtor, "Do you think the owner might consider selling the bed?"

Her response surprised me. "I think he may be interested in selling all the furniture. Why don't you e-mail him?" The thought of purchasing the whole house full of furniture was definitely attractive. Every room was tastefully decorated, and there were some pieces of furniture that were especially appealing, like the lighted china cabinet, the handsome buffet, the huge desk, and the comfy sofa and recliner. Ah, yes, I'd like to have every piece, but the odds of being able to afford the entire collection of furniture seemed pretty slim. Nevertheless, I e-mailed the owner and asked him to break down the cost of the furniture room by room.

The e-mail I received in return made me blink my eyes in disbelief. The price he quoted for all the furniture and appliances (including a large washer and dryer and two televisions) was about one-fifth of what I expected. I jumped at the chance and bought everything. My house was move-in ready!

All I lacked were morning and evening helpers. Mama stayed with me for a while as I searched for just the right persons to care for me. Finally I found Alvinas and Effie.

Alvinas ("Al"), a sweet lady in her sixties, had a broad smile and a gentle, grandmotherly way about her. Al picked me up from work in the afternoons, fed me dinner, straightened up around the house, and then helped me take a shower and get ready for bed before she left at 9 o'clock. She was a fantastic cook, and often she would bring me some of her home cooking,

Al had little formal education. In fact, one evening she confided her embarrassment over not being able to read very well. Nevertheless, I came to realize the vast amounts of down-to-earth wisdom and goodness that Al possessed. She said, "I always get to your office a little early to pick you up because I never want you to be afraid that I'm not coming. And I always try to get your supper ready in a hurry because I know you don't take time to eat much lunch and you must be hungry." She always had my well-being at heart.

Al was nearly as excited as I was when I got my border collie, Sonny. They bonded immediately, and often Al would cup Sonny's face in her hands and gently rub his head.

Shortly after I had to move back home, Al developed terminal cancer and died very soon. I still miss her today and wish I had one more chance to sit at her feet and learn the lessons that life had taught her.

Effie, my morning helper, was about my age. Like Al, Effie was kind and dependable. She arrived at 7 o'clock every morning, fed me breakfast, got me ready for work, and drove me to my office. Effie had an eye for fashion, and she liked helping me put together outfits. Mostly, we just enjoyed our morning chats.

Effie was always willing to come to my rescue when I needed out-of-the-ordinary help. One morning Effie arrived at my house to find me extremely ill. She took me to the emergency room, where Kathleen met us. They both waited with me until I was released, even though it meant that Effie was late for her other job.

Effie later married and moved to St. Louis. We still talk from time to time, though I miss the closeness we had when I saw her every day.

A wonderful young lady named Pam took Effie's place. Pam, too, had an extraordinary kindness and sensitivity to my needs. Although she was with me for only a short time, we grew very close. She sent me cards and letters that made our friendship continue.

Without the devotion of these exceptional ladies, I could not possibly have lived in Oxford in my own house. God sent them my way, and I will be forever grateful for the care and friendship with which they blessed me.

Sonny, My Sunshine

The e-mail came on February 11, 2002. It was brief and said only, "I have a six-month male that is black and white with the best ever temperament. He only wants to please you. He always is under foot or would be in your lap. I would be honored if you would be his Mom. Would you be able to speak with me? Attached is a picture of Sonny."

Lisa was replying to an e-mail I had sent to her on a whim, asking if she had a 6-to-9-month-old Border Collie puppy that I could train as a service dog. I had heard how brilliant Border Collies are, so I had searched the Internet for a breeder and had found Lisa in Florence, Alabama. After receiving her e-mail, I phoned her.

I could sense an excitement in Lisa's voice as she told me that she had the perfect little guy for me. The story behind Sonny left me awestruck. He was originally scheduled to be shipped overseas, but the 9/11 crisis prevented any airline shipment of dogs; so Lisa had kept him and raised him as her pet for the first six months of his life. Lisa went on to tell me that she had had a daughter with cerebral palsy who had died at age 12 and that her kennels (JuleToo Farms) were named for her daughter Julie. Sonny was Lisa's special pet, but she wanted me to have him as a token of the work she had begun in honor of Julie.

The following Saturday some friends drove me to Florence to get Sonny. We arrived at a beautiful farm, with green fields, ponds, swans, and sheep – a heavenly place to raise dogs. Lisa emerged from the farmhouse and immediately hugged me tightly. We were both keenly aware of the bond we shared through Julie.

Running through the yard was a myriad of black-and-white pups. Lisa brought Sonny over to me and introduced us. I reached down to pet Sonny, all the while wondering how long it would take him to accept me as his new Mom. Lisa let us watch as the dogs played Frisbee. She explained, "Sonny is always the one who hangs back. He'll let one of the other dogs catch the Frisbee almost every time." She was right. Sonny has a soft temperament that avoids conflict.

We soon went into the farmhouse, where Sonny and I could get acquainted. I noticed a picture of Julie on the mantel. She had a delicately sweet face and beautiful blond hair worn in pigtails. I could only imagine the pain of losing her.

In the middle of the living room there was an oversized lounge chair. "That's where I sit and rock Sonny," Lisa said. "Would you like to sit there and hold him?" Eagerly assenting, I asked my friends to help me into the chair. But before Lisa could bring Sonny to me, I began sliding out of the chair. "I know what to do," said Lisa as she ran to get pillows to prop me up. I could sense that she was pleased at how quickly it all came back to her.

Once I was settled in the chair, Lisa placed Sonny in my lap. Even though he didn't know me, he seemed content with me. A friend of Lisa came in and saw me with Sonny. Looking at Lisa, she said, "I can't believe you're not crying." Lisa replied, "Oh, I did that all morning, before they got here." I began to wonder how I could take Sonny away.

We went outside again and watched the puppies play. I was delaying the inevitable. It was Lisa who finally said, "It's getting late, and you have a long drive. You really need to be going. I've played with Sonny all day so he would be tired and hopefully sleep most of the way back."

I had brought a crate for Sonny, but I didn't put him in it. Instead, my friends took me out of my chair and set me on the back seat, with Sonny beside me. I was worried that he might whimper upon leaving Lisa, but he seemed to know he was going to his new home. I stroked him gently most of the way home.

When we got home with Sonny, everybody was waiting to greet the new arrival. It was almost like bringing home a new baby. He adjusted well and began going to work with me, as well as working with a trainer (my friend Tammy) to learn skills that would help me.

Sonny makes people of all ages smile; and when he is with individuals who are a little shy or reserved, he brings them out and makes them feel as special as they are. In playing the role of ice breaker, he has helped me to overcome some of the isolation that is an inevitable consequence of being in a wheelchair.

Sonny is able to understand my speech as though it were crystal clear (which it is to him). He is a pure delight to have in my life and in the lives of my family and friends. He is my constant companion. He's known all over the Ole Miss campus and is kind of the mascot in Guyton Hall. Sonny is a "people dog," liking to shake hands and greet people with his own special warmth. He is eager to please and has such a magnetic personality that he makes everyone feel at ease and welcome.

My e-mails to Lisa went something like this:

July 13, 2002
Hello, Lisa,

I think about you so often as I watch Sonny grow and mature. He's a handsome fellow, and everywhere I go, people comment on his beauty. Even more wonder-

ful, he has the sweetest disposition. When he wants something, he just sits and looks at me with those big brown eyes, and he waits so patiently while I get what he wants. He understands so much! One night a doorbell rang on TV, and Sonny looked at the front door. I said, "No, sweetie, that was on TV." And he looked at the TV!

I love taking him places. Today we went to a 4-H horse competition. He loved watching the horses.

It's late now, and he's in his usual place -- right here under my desk. When I go to bed, he'll follow me there.

He has started working on the higher level helping tasks, like learning to pick up things I drop. He likes learning and is so eager to please. He's going to be a great service dog, but even more importantly, he's already a great companion.

We're already planning his birthday party! I'm hoping he'll wear a birthday hat long enough for a picture. I'll send you one.

I hope all is well with you. I'll forever remember and be grateful for your kindness and generosity in letting me be Sonny's second mom. He enriches my life more than I can tell you, and I feel that a part of you and a part of Julie lives in him and makes him all the more special.

Then on February 27, 2003, I wrote:

Hi, Lisa - I hope you're doing well. Sonny and I are doing fine. Sonny is sooo sweet and smart. He loves to shake hands with people (and that immediately endears him to everyone). He's learning to help me more all the time. He can turn on my touch lamp for me when I say, "Sonny, light." He can "take" things from the floor and put them in my lap. He's also learning to open the door by pulling on a towel hung on the lever. I wish you could see him walking down the hall with me at work. He doesn't even need a leash there any more. He walks so proudly, with his tail up like a flag. If he gets a little ahead, he'll look back to be sure I'm coming. He walks straight as an arrow right to my office. At home he loves to play Frisbee and to put one foot in his dish and skate across the patio. We plan to get a video of that, and I'll send one to you. As you can tell, he enriches my life so much. He's funny, charming, witty, and beautiful -- and he knows it! Well, I could go on and on, but you know what a special little guy he is. I've had many people say he must have been sent from God -- yes, through one of His angels named Julie. Thank you, Lisa, forever and always for saving Sonny just for me!

In September 2004, I wrote:

Sonny is doing great! He amazes everyone -- and, oh, what a charmer he is! His latest trick was to crawl under the "occupied" handicapped stall in the ladies restroom! I had NO idea who was in there, but a friend of mine came out laughing. Apparently he knew her smell and just went in to say hello!

In February 2006, I wrote:

I want you to know how well Sonny continues to do. He has lots of friends here and at Ole Miss, and some of the pretty girls at work have started taking him walking with them. He loves that, and so do they! One day, one of the professors found Sonny in the hall and asked me if he needed to go out. I said, "I don't think so. What is he doing?" He said, "Chasing girls!" Anyway, he's a pleasure to me and to everyone else.

At the end of October 2007, I wrote:

Our Sonny boy turned 6 in July, and he never ceases to amaze me. Every time I think he can't get any sweeter or smarter, he fools me. Everyone who spends any time with him is convinced he's human. He still goes to work with me every day, and I have several people who take him walking for me. One of them is a little 11-year-old girl who had told her mother that she wanted a job walking a dog! Another of his walkers is a guy who takes him on adventures in the woods.

At night we've taught him to play hide and seek. He "stays" while my helper hides treats around the house. Then he goes and finds them! He caught onto that game in a hurry, and now he begs to play it.

I love having Sonny with me all the time. I love being able to reach over and pet him when we're in bed. Sometimes he'll lay his head on my stomach and look at me with those big brown eyes.

I'm grateful for him -- and you -- every single day.

On January 11, 2009, I wrote:

I hope you got the pictures of Sonny. I wanted to tell you more about him. He really isn't a service dog because he isn't exactly a dog. I can't explain, except to say that everyone who gets to know him says, without prompting, "He acts human, like a little boy." Lisa, I guess God knew how much I wanted a child, and that's what Sonny has turned out to be. He has lots of toys, and the other day I said, "Sonny, come move your elephant out of Mommy's way." He came and got his elephant. And one day he was in the restroom with me at work, and he laid his head on my knee and looked me right in the eye. I knew exactly what he was saying, so I told him, "Okay, as soon as I go potty, I'll take you to go potty." Sure enough, that's what he wanted. He's so proud of his job of being my little boy. He knows my name as "Mama." And I truly believe that God and Sonny got together and decided how Sonny could help me best, and it was in a way that no one would ever think of. How neat is that!

We love you,
Maxine & Sonny (perfect name!)

Guyton Hall and Job Promotions

The year 2003 proved to be a time of exciting changes in my job at Ole Miss. Most importantly, I was promoted to Associate Director of the Center for Educational Research and Evaluation (which we call CERE), where I had worked for the past three years. Secondly, I was made an adjunct faculty member, being asked to teach an online course in "Introduction to Special Education."

These career advances reinforced my belief that I was a useful and productive member of the academic community. In 2004, I was named the Outstanding Faculty Researcher by the University of Mississippi chapter of Phi Delta Kappa. I was excited by all that I was learning and doing. My work filled that strong need I have always had to live up to my fullest potential.

Remember my "book closet" office? Well, in January 2004, the School of Education moved into the newly renovated Guyton Hall, and I had a gorgeous new office – triple the size of the old one, with two large windows. Best of all, Kathleen's office was right next door!

One day soon after I had moved into my new office, Mama and Daddy came to visit. I didn't hear them when they came into the main door of the building, but Sonny did! He ran to greet them; and since they didn't know the way to my office, Sonny led them – all the while looking back to be sure they were following.

That spring the School of Education was interviewing for a new Dean. I was sitting with the other faculty members in the large meeting room when in walked Tom – yes, the Tom from my Delta State days. He didn't see me at first; but then he turned and spotted me. A look of total surprise crossed his face, and he smiled and gave me a hug. Tom assumed the position of Dean in July 2004. But he never forgot his "position" as my friend.

Kathleen and I continued to work closely together – almost seamlessly. We knew each other's thought patterns, each other's preferences. Together we wrote evaluation proposals; we collected and analyzed data; and we wrote technical reports of our findings. I learned the art of evaluation from the master.

Kathleen had warned me that she would retire one day. That day came at the end of June 2006. Barb became Director of CERE, and I continued as Associate Director. Barb and I worked well together, too, and Barb always kept a jar of treats in her office for Sonny.

One day in June 2008, Barb called me into her office. Thinking that she wanted to discuss a proposal we were working on, I took a draft of the proposal in with me. To my surprise, Barb laid the proposal down and said, "I've decided to step down and pursue my real love – mathematics education. I've recommended to the Dean that you move up to the Director's position."

And so it was that in July 2008, I became Interim Director of CERE. It's funny how natural it felt. After 8 years, this was "my" center. I was intimately acquainted with every proposal we had written, every piece of data we had analyzed, and every report we had compiled. I could see the succession – how we broadened our scope, refined our techniques, developed our own patterns.

Over those 8 years I changed, too – from a novice who had everything to learn, to a confident leader who had lots to teach. At the May 2008 graduation, I received the Outstanding Grant Writing Award, bestowed by the School of Education.

Without diminishing my love for my work, it has always been the people who have made the work enjoyable – and productive. Whoever coined the term "right hand man" must have had in mind Joey, my Project Coordinator, and the many graduate assistants with whom I've had the privilege of working. Each person has carved a special place in my heart. I wish I could name every one who has come my way, but you know who you are (Sherry, April, Susan, Kathryn, Angela, Jill, Gerilynn, and the list goes on). You must know that I could not have done my job without you. Every day I looked forward to your coming into my office and bringing your own unique personalities, your own special gifts, to grace my efforts. "Teamwork" finds its highest fulfillment inside the walls of 134 Guyton Hall.

Someone Named April

She walked into my office one day early in the fall semester of 2001. She introduced herself as April and said that she had come to apply for a work-study position. I noticed how pretty she was, with her long, dark hair and her sparkling white teeth. During our conversation, I learned that she was a junior and that her major was accounting. "Hmm, she must be pretty smart," I mused to myself. But I didn't learn much more about April during that initial interview. She seemed shy, and I wondered whether she would really come to work for me or whether my CP-wracked body had turned her away.

To my delight, April did come back the next day – and the next. Whatever I had perceived as shyness quickly faded as she fell into the routine of helping me. My first impression – that she was bright – proved to be abundantly true. She caught on quickly to everything we did, whether it was tedious tables or complicated spreadsheets. I was always amazed at how quickly she got things done. If her designated time to leave was 4:00, she would somehow finish the task she was working on at exactly 4:00.

April's beauty and intelligence were striking, but her personality was even more striking. She'd bee-bop into my office as happy as could be, always smiling. Even the ringtone on her cell phone reflected her cheerful spirit. It sounded like beach music. Her smile was contagious. It made me happy.

April developed an unusual sense of responsibility toward me. If she was with me at lunch time, she would feed me. I remember one day in particular when I'd had very little time to eat. As I raced out the door to a meeting, April said, "Here, eat just one more chicken nugget." Also keenly aware of my precarious balance, April was visibly upset the day my wheelchair stopped working and she had to leave me in a regular rolling chair when she went to class. Seeing the look of dismay on April's face, a classmate asked her what on earth was wrong. She wailed, "I had to take Maxine out of her chair and put her in another one, and I'm afraid she's gonna fall out."

April came to my house many nights to help me grade papers or catch up on other work. Her presence was a sure cure for the loneliness that so often invaded my life. As the days passed, I grew more and more attached to April. She helped me see Sonny through his puppyhood, and she stood by me even when my legs began to fail me.

To my great delight, April remained with me through her junior and senior years, then through her year in graduate school. She became like a daughter to me, and I dreaded the time when she would leave me. That day came in

July 2004. Everyone was worried that I wouldn't be able to contain the tears. I managed, though, to keep smiling as I hugged April good-bye.

I've talked with April on the phone several times since she graduated. Her accounting career has kept her working long hours. To this day, I still miss her, and something tells me I always will.

Divine Connections

Her eyes never left my face during the entire hour I spoke. She was a student earning a degree in education, and I had been asked to speak to her class that night about my experiences as a child and as an adult with cerebral palsy. I talked about having to overcome others' preconceived notions of all the things I would never be able to do. I told about the director of the residential facility who warned my parents, in my presence, not to expect me to ever be able to attend a regular school. Wouldn't he be surprised if he were alive today!

When I spoke to classes such as this one, it wasn't unusual for some students to be much more interested than others in what I was saying; but I sensed something different about this particular student – this one who seemed so intent on catching every word I said. I knew she would come up and talk with me later, during the break, but I had no idea what she would say.

During the question and answer period, other students shared stories that surprised and touched me. One, whose child had a severe hearing impairment, told how painful it was for the "professionals" to tell her only what her son couldn't do, never what his potential was. "Now," she said, "you've helped me see how important it is for me to recognize his abilities and not allow others to focus only on his weaknesses. Thank you for that."

Another student raised her hand and smiled. "I have dyslexia," she said. "When I was in elementary school, my mother had to fight against having me placed in special education. Even my uncle thought I would flunk out of school. But I worked hard and graduated in the top third of my class. Then I got my Associate Degree, and now I'm working on my Bachelor's Degree in Education. Hearing you speak made me believe more than ever that I can do anything I put my mind to, and that I shouldn't let anyone dissuade me from pursuing my dreams."

It was later that the first student told me her story. "Seeing you and hearing about your life brought it all back," she said. "I had a little girl who aspirated amniotic fluid during birth and was left with brain damage. The doctors said she'd never walk or talk and probably wouldn't live long anyway, so we should just put her away and go on with our lives. My husband and I decided, though, that if all she could ever do was lie there and look pretty, that would be enough for us. So we took her home. We were feeding her through an NG tube, but neither she nor I got any pleasure from that, so I decided to try giving her a bottle. A speech therapist taught me how to hold my finger under her lower lip and help her suck. She caught on to that really fast and gained about 15 pounds in three months. Even though she never talked, she smiled and even laughed out loud a few times. I was even teaching her to stand holding onto my hands. Despite the early predictions that she might live only a few weeks, she lived three wonderful years. But she kept having pneumonia, and her lungs finally gave out. She died one night in her sleep. I'm happy for the time we had with her, and I'm happy to hear what you've accomplished in your lifetime."

I left the class that night with a profound sense of awe at the ways in which God chooses to connect our lives and help us see each other through His eyes.

On That Day

I really didn't know how much freedom I had – until I lost it. For years I had been able to use the restroom by myself and get in and out of bed by myself. Oh, what luxuries those were! It meant I could live alone – stay by myself at night, go to bed whenever I pleased, and get up anytime I needed to (or wanted to). Sometimes I would go out with Sonny at 3 a.m. and just stare in awe at the moon and stars.

My back door with its glass panes was my tiny chapel where I would have my visits with God, usually late at night when the rest of the world was quiet and I could see the tree branches against the dark night sky. I was free to pray out loud or even sing, with no one except God to hear. I knew He understood every broken word, and I knew my singing was music to His ears, if to no others'.

My health had been incredibly good throughout my 30s. I was rarely sick, and even then I had "normal" illnesses – a sore throat, a stomach bug, nothing more. But when I was in my early 40s, I began having severe pain in my joints. For a while, the doctors attributed the pain to the cerebral palsy. Then they did blood work that showed I had rheumatoid arthritis, an unbelievably debilitating condition for even ordinary people, and no one had ever heard of the combination of cerebral palsy and rheumatoid arthritis. But I had it. I wish my odds had been equally as good at a lottery as they were lousy at medical occurrences.

Despite the added complication of the rheumatoid arthritis, I continued to be able to live alone – that is, until the day when the loss of cartilage in my knees stopped my legs from being able to support my weight. It felt strange. I would grab the rail in my usual manner and try to pull myself up, only to have my knees crumble under me.

Visits to several orthopedic surgeons revealed that the constant tension from the cerebral palsy, combined with the arthritis in my joints, had stripped the cartilage from my knees, leaving bone rubbing against bone. In fact, a radiologist at the office of one of the orthopedic surgeons looked at my X-rays and said, almost with tears in his eyes, "Your legs hurt you a lot, don't they?"

The doctors and therapists tried several treatments, including cortisone injections, ultrasound, and electrical stimulation; but nothing seemed to help. What I really needed was a knee replacement; but that required being able to straighten my knees out fully and go through rigorous rehabilitation therapy, neither of which was possible for me. Unless I could meet these criteria, I would be in serious danger of developing deadly blood clots. One of the orthopedic surgeons remarked, "I am so sorry. But no one in their right mind would perform knee replacement surgery on you. You would not survive."

And so it was that the tiny bit of independence I had enjoyed ceased to be. Ever after, I would need help using the restroom and getting in and out of bed. My parents moved into my house to help as much as they could, and others (primarily Wanda) began helping me get into and out of bed.

On that one day, everything changed.

The Pump

"Why did you let yourself get like this?" one of the orthopedic surgeons asked. I looked at him in disbelief that he could be so heartless. I choked back the tears and looked him square in the eyes and said, "Look, I have been dealing with this for 50 years, and I have been doing the very best I could. Can you tell me what I could have done differently?"

The arrogant doctor looked puzzled and said nothing. Later I wished that I had responded to his question by saying, "An idiot like you delivered me."

He was one in a long line of specialists that I saw after that eventful day when my legs stopped working and I could no longer transfer myself from my chair to my bed or to any other place – that one day when I lost what tiny bit of independence I had. For a long time I was determined to gain that independence back, no matter what it took.

To make matters worse, I later began having severe muscle cramps in my legs, so severe that I would scream out during the night and Daddy would have to come and help me hang my legs off the side of the bed. A specialist finally diagnosed the problem as degenerative disc disease.

A pain management specialist prescribed spinal injections to halt the horrible spasms. I distinctly remember the first of these injections. When I arrived at the pain clinic several hours away, a kind nurse helped me into a gown, and another nurse inserted an IV into my arm. Then I rolled down the hall to the procedure room. The male nurse who assisted with the procedure wanted to lay me down on the table. At that time, having my legs in a forward position was excruciating, so he kindly agreed to let me sit on the edge of the table until they put me to sleep.

A few minutes later, I awoke with the strangest feeling. There was no pain, no spasticity – just complete relaxation like I had never felt. I thought for a moment that I had died and gone to heaven. My mother and sister described the look on my face as one of such surprise. They couldn't figure out what the look meant. That incredible feeling of total relaxation lasted perhaps sixty seconds. Then, gradually, stealthily, the demon returned, and I was spastic again. Yep, I was alive.

The good news was that the injection did stop the horrible spasms. Unfortunately, the injections lasted only a few months; then the pain returned. At that point, I became willing to try almost anything.

The doctors began talking with me about the baclofen pump – a device that is implanted to deliver muscle relaxant medicine to the spine. It was touted to be the panacea for my problem – the one possibility for giving me back my independence.

I spoke to a representative from the company that makes the device, and she gave me a million reasons why I should opt for the surgery. She eagerly helped me schedule an appointment with a neurosurgeon that commonly performed this type of surgery. When I saw him, my meeting was brief, probably fifteen minutes long. He explained a little about the surgery and arranged for me to have the trial done the following week, then the surgery the day after. The purpose of the trial was to introduce a single dose of the baclofen into my spine and see what effect it had over several hours.

Having heard no negatives about the surgery, I agreed to have the trial scheduled for the following week. I was anxious to have the surgery behind me by the time my cousins arrived for our big Thanksgiving reunion. The prospect of seeing my family gave me something to look forward to after the surgery.

I tied up all my loose ends at work and prepared to be away for a couple of weeks. I had to admit that even though everyone had said that the surgery was minor, I was still nervous – no, scared. I tried hard to focus on a wonderful outcome and not on the pain of the surgery.

I intentionally kept myself busy until the moment of departure. Knowing that I would be away for a week, I found it hard to leave Sonny. My cousin Emmy made arrangements to take my mother and me to the hospital several hours away and stay with me until Wanda could come and relieve her.

I entered the hospital on a Monday evening. The trial was scheduled for early Tuesday morning, early enough that my reaction to the trial could be checked throughout the day. However, there was a four hour delay in beginning the trial. It was around noon when the neurosurgeon finally met me in the operating room and injected a small amount of baclofen into my spine.

Over the next few hours, a physical therapist monitored my spasticity level to see whether the baclofen was having the desired effect. Actually, I was able to distinguish myself the differences in the way I felt. My back was straighter, I sat more comfortably in my chair, and even my speech seemed clearer and less strained. I was elated. So when the neurosurgeon came around that night, we decided that the trial had been a success and that the surgery would go forward the next day. I was to be first on the list.

Unfortunately, that evening the trial dose of medicine wore off and the muscle cramps from my pinched nerve returned with a vengeance. I begged for pain killers, but the nurses refused, saying that they were not on my orders for the night. The only way I could bear the pain was to sit in my chair for the rest of the night.

Finally, around 5 a.m., I asked my mother to call Emmy to come from the motel and help me. Emmy said later that when she walked into my room, I looked like a deer caught in the headlights. She remembers praying that God would show her what to do. She got on her knees at my feet and began massaging my leg up and down, up and down. Miraculously, the pain eased until it was at least bearable.

I thought I would be going to surgery in just another hour or so, but the staff had gotten me confused with another patient and had taken the other patient first. So I had to wait. When I finally got to the operating room, the spasms were out the roof and I was begging to be put out. "We have a problem with your IV," the operating room nurse said, "and we have to change it out." I didn't know how I could hang on that long.

"Can't you put me out first, then change the IV?" I pleaded. No go. The IV had to be changed. When that was done, the surgeon still had not come into the operating room. The anesthesiologist took pity on me and said, "Let's go ahead and put her out." That's the last thing I remember.

I woke up in my room. My first instinct told me that the surgery had been more difficult on my body than I had anticipated. I was terribly weak and in more pain than I was expecting. A nurse came in and gave me a shot to lessen the pain. But the shot made me groggy and almost unable to speak.

My friend Jim called to see how I was doing. My mother let me speak to him, and he later said that he was frightened by the way I sounded. My friend Marsha's mother came to check on me and immediately called Marsha and said, "She isn't doing very well."

Strange things were happening. I was too weak to drink from a straw, so Wanda figured out a way to trap the liquid in the straw by holding her finger over the hole and then releasing the liquid into my mouth. My pills had to be crushed, too; so giving my medicine took a really long time. At one point, Wanda told the nurse, "You can leave the medicine and I'll give it to her. I don't want you to have to wait." Oddly the nurse replied, "I have to watch her take it because sometimes family members steal medicine." Wanda still laughs about that and says, "I guess she didn't know I had had at least 30 years to swipe your medicine."

I remember one nurse especially well. She stayed after her shift to catheterize me because no one else had been successful, and I was suffering from the need to eliminate fluid. I knew she was tired from her 12 hour shift, but she still had compassion for my predicament. My memories are sporadic, but I also remember Emmy stashing away the one type of catheter that they had found that would work with me.

Another surprise for me was waking up and seeing the pump in my left side. The thing was huge. I had been told that it would be barely visible, but I felt like I was carrying around a can of Skoal tobacco. Although I was certainly an adult, I was more the size of a teenager, so this device looked and felt like it was going to burst through my skin.

The incision in my side was about three inches long, and the one in my back was about five inches long. My back hurt much worse than my side, and it was a few days before I could sit up comfortably.

I stayed on the surgery floor for three days; then I was moved to the rehabilitation unit. I must say that my experience there was rather bizarre. I was "evaluated" by therapists who apparently thought I was there to gain some skills, when I was actually there only to get relief from pain. Their methods confused and frightened me.

First, they set me on a cot and examined the range of motion in my arms and legs. The range wasn't much. My right wrist was frozen in a downward position. One of the therapists proclaimed, "We're going to straighten that wrist out," to which I replied, "Oh, no, you're not!" Next, one of the therapists announced, "We're going to teach you to sit alone." Since I had never sat alone in the 49 years of my life, I wondered how they were going to accomplish that feat. Then came the grandmother of all questions – "How long has it been since you've cooked a meal?"

I finally asked to be released from the circus and taken back to my room. My mother and Wanda were waiting there. I looked Wanda square in the eyes and said, "Get me the hell out of here before they kill me." Wanda smiled and said, "I think I saw the neurologist at the desk. Why don't you go and talk to him?" I practically raced down the hall and wheeled up to the nurse's station. Sure enough, the doctor was sitting there making notes on charts. I said with a quizzical look, "I don't think I'm supposed to be in this unit. They're trying to train me to do some stupid stuff that I've never been able to do in my whole life, and I don't think this surgery was that much of a miracle." Surprisingly enough, the doctor agreed, "You should never have been put in the rehabilitation unit. I'll sign the papers, and you can go home tomorrow." I smiled and said, "Thanks."

Even surgery couldn't stop me from shopping. My mother's cousin Joan came to visit me, and I went AWOL with her. I had lost my shoes and needed some more, so we sneaked out of the hospital and went to a Payless shoe store nearby. We got caught. When I got back to the hospital, the doctor wanted to see my pass (really!). Didn't have one. OK, arrest me. Jail would be better than this place.

My recovery was hindered by the fact that my pinched nerve caused by the degenerative disc disease was still causing me agony, and the pain specialist couldn't do another spinal injection until at least a week had passed after my surgery. The doctor tried to lessen the discomfort with a drug for nerve pain. It helped some, but it made me very groggy. Sometimes I would fall asleep between the time my mother put the spoon in the dish and the time she got it to my mouth.

Finally, on Monday, my cousin Phil came to bring me home. As he drove, he kept his eye on me through the rearview mirror. He had to stop three times to pull me back into my chair because I kept falling asleep and sliding out.

The week following was a fog because the pain medicine kept me asleep most of the time. I continued to have the horrible spasms in my legs; they would not go away until I could have another spinal injection. Finally, on Friday I was able to make the long trek back to the pain clinic and have the injection.

Afterward, I went to the surgeon's office to have my stitches removed. I expected some pain, but nothing like what happened. The stitches in my lower back had gone in crooked and had to be virtually ripped out of my back. In fact, some of the incision was re-opened. The pain was almost unbearable. However, the nurse did not attempt to deaden the area or to make the procedure less painful. Later, I saw on my medical records the statement, "Stitches were removed without incident or complications." I guess the incident was only on my end.

The torment was finally over, and I could focus on recovering. Daddy had not seen my incisions, and one night he had to dress them for me. He dressed my side first, which wasn't too bad. Then he dressed my back. When he saw the size of both incisions, he said "Honey, they ripped you up good, didn't they?" The look in his eyes was one of deep sorrow. I said, "Yeah, but it's OK; I'll be fine."

I was longing to return to work, to some place where I felt normal again. It was about three weeks after my surgery when my van pulled up to Guyton Hall once again. I was greeted with hugs and smiles of welcome. Even though I was anxious to get back into the full swing of work, I was surprised at how weak I was. I was able to stay for only part of the day for the next two or three weeks. Thanksgiving came soon, and along with it the big family reunion for which I had been waiting. Relatives began arriving on Tuesday. Lauri Anne walked in the back door with her arms open wide to hug me. Then she stopped and said, "Oops, where is it ok to hug you?" At that moment, anywhere was just fine.

Hurricanes

While Hurricane Katrina was forming over the Bahamas on August 23, 2005, I was battling my own hurricane in an operating room. This personal hurricane, the breaking of the medicine-carrying catheter in my spine, began brewing on Thursday, July 21, 2005 – approximately 9 months after the apparatus had been surgically implanted. Ironically, I was in New Orleans, where I had gone with my cousin Emmy and friend Shirley to see a neurosurgical specialist about my pump. A second medicine had been added to the baclofen pump in an effort to ease the relentless pain in my legs, but now everything seemed out of kilter.

My appointment with the specialist on Wednesday, July 20th, ran late. The doctor was an interesting fellow, probably between 65 and 70 years old. We chided him for staying so late when he probably had a family waiting for him at home. "Nope," he said. "In all my years of practice, I've only met one neurosurgeon who remained married throughout his career. The profession is just too demanding. I was a pediatric neurosurgeon for a while, but I burned out and had to turn it over to someone younger. You just see too many sad cases that you can't fix."

Little did any of us know that I was a case that he wouldn't have an opportunity to fix. He looked at the CT scan I had brought with me and said there was a problem with the catheter. It needed to be replaced. He scheduled surgery for August 4th. I didn't make it to August 4th; in fact, I almost didn't make it at all.

After the appointment, we ate and went back to the hotel. I made phone calls to family and friends with the surprising news, "The neurosurgeon says the catheter is in the wrong place, and he wants to operate on August 4th and replace it." Somehow I felt a sense of relief that my instincts had been proven right – something had indeed gone wrong with the pump. However, the prospect of another surgery didn't please me at all. The little sleep I was able to get on Wednesday night was fitful, not at all restful. I had a slight headache and just an overall ill feeling, but I had no idea what was causing it.

We got up on Thursday morning and decided to putter around New Orleans before returning home. My headache had intensified, and the steaming heat only made it worse. We strolled through the French Quarter and stopped at Café Du Monde for a mid-morning breakfast of beignets. Normally a doughnut lover, I found I had no appetite that morning, even for beignets. I just wanted my Coke.

After leaving the café, we caught a trolley car to travel through downtown New Orleans. It happened to be the one – the only one – with no air conditioning. An ideal place, I thought, to make a drunk with a hangover swear never to drink again – well, swear anyway!

We left New Orleans late that afternoon. All the way home, I had Shirley turning the air conditioner in the van up and down, up and down, as my body temperature turned from hot to cold and back to hot again. When we dropped Emmy off at her house, I asked her for an empty Cool Whip container. She knew what it was for. I thought then that I had a sinus infection that was making me so sick. Little did I know that it was so much worse.

I remember almost nothing about the weekend. Since my summer online class was almost over, I surely must have graded papers, but I don't remember doing it. There was an important meeting at work on Monday, so I went even though I felt really strange. Kathleen made me come home immediately after the meeting. I was too sick to put up a fight.

By Tuesday, I knew I was in trouble. And I knew what it was – withdrawal! I was shaking uncontrollably. The doctor said it would pass – I just had to bear with it for a little while. But as the day wore on, I got worse. Then the pain set in. My legs became contorted with pain, more pain than I ever dreamed possible. I took morphine and baclofen by mouth. Nothing helped.

Shirley, my friend and helper, wouldn't leave me. Somehow she got me into bed, I don't remember how. Other friends began coming and going, but I couldn't focus because the pain was too intense. I said over and over, "I can't handle the pain. I can't handle it." I believed this was the end; I was dying. Daddy was sitting beside me on the bed gently rubbing my legs. I remember saying to him, "I have to go. Thank you for bringing me up so that I'm not afraid to go. Please don't be disappointed in me."

It was a strange feeling, though, to be so suddenly faced with the prospect of dying. "What is heaven like, dear God?" I asked. The answer that came to me was one I hadn't expected. "I can't tell you, my child. It's beyond your comprehension. I can only tell you that no one ever asks to come back to this earth."

Time passed slowly, eerily. I couldn't believe I was still alive and in that much pain. "It's not possible," I thought. God was my friend. He loved me. He wouldn't leave me in that much pain. Yet the pain was relentless, indescribably horrific. The verse came to mind, "My God, my God, why hast thou forsaken me?" (Matthew 27:46)

Wanda and Avent were on vacation at the beach. I asked Mama to call Wanda and tell her I was in withdrawal and was very sick, but I didn't want her to cut her vacation short and come home. Quite honestly, I didn't think she could get here in time anyway.

Everyone urged me to go to the hospital; but I resisted, thinking that our local hospital knew nothing about the pump. Besides, in my mind I was dying, and I wanted to die at home.

Finally, around midnight, Daddy made one last plea. "Please, please go to the hospital and see what they can do." At last I consented. In a few minutes I saw flashing lights through my bedroom window as the ambulance pulled into the driveway. The EMTs came in and transferred me from my bed to a gurney. They tried to be gentle, but any movement at all was sheer torture.

Then, as the EMTs wheeled the gurney through the living room, I vaguely realized that Sonny hadn't tried to get between these strangers and me; nor had he barked as he usually did when strangers entered the house. I looked around to see where he was, and that's when my heart broke. Sonny was sitting in a corner of the living room, totally out of the way, crying.

I wanted Shirley to ride with me in the ambulance. She could understand what I said; and best of all, she would make them be gentle with my legs. The ambulance ride was short but oh, so hot. Mama and my friend and helper Wanda followed in the car.

I remember little about the emergency room except that the doctor said my white count was extremely high. I only wanted the pain to stop. I kept saying, "I want to go home." I meant my home in heaven.

My own internist was out of town for the remainder of the week. The doctor who filled in was kind and compassionate, sincerely wanting to help; but my condition deteriorated nonetheless. I was placed on a morphine pump, the kind that's used to relieve severe post-operative pain. It's programmed to deliver a small dose of morphine when the patient pushes the button, as long as enough time has lapsed between each pressing of the button. I think mine was programmed to allow me a drop every five minutes. Of course, someone had to push the button for me, and I was constantly begging for it to be pushed. The morphine took the edge off the pain for a few seconds, but did little more.

I learned later that the doctor had asked if I wanted more painkiller. Although I don't remember it, he explained that if he upped the morphine enough so that the pain would stop, my breathing might stop, too. I don't think I was coherent enough to understand or reply. In any case, they didn't turn the morphine up.

Wanda and Avent came home early from their vacation. My condition continued to worsen. Despite intensive intravenous antibiotics, my white count remained sky high. Eating and drinking were basically out of the question. The doctor asked if I wanted a feeding tube. I shook my head and said no.

On Saturday, my cousin Lisa, an internist in Dallas, arrived. She and a high school friend who was a surgeon at the local hospital looked at the CT scan of my catheter and discussed the possibility of removing the faulty catheter. The surgeon decided that it would be too risky.

Lisa stayed with me in the hospital that night. By that time I was gravely ill, believing that death must be imminent. "Lisa," I said, my voice barely above a whisper, "did I do it right? I tried, I really tried, but did I do it right?"

Lisa smiled, almost laughed. "Honey," she said, "you don't need to worry about that. You did it just right." I told her that all I really wanted was to hear my Lord say, "Well done, my good and faithful servant." When Lisa left the next day, I wasn't sure I would see her again this side of heaven.

My internist returned from vacation on Monday. He walked into my hospital room, pulled up a chair beside my bed and began glancing over my chart. I thought he looked worried. He teased, "Why did you have to get sick while I was out of town?" My mother shot back, "Why did you have to leave town when she was sick?"

My doctor ordered IV steroids. I learned later that the horrible withdrawal had sent my immune system into a tailspin, making my white count soar. The steroids were given in an effort to shock my immune system back into operation. Pain continued to wrack my body. I had hoped to finally get better without dealing with the pump. I wanted nothing more to do with it, but it became clear that I was sorely dependent on it. Perhaps if I just had it refilled, that would fix the problem. But my doctor's reply was, "She's too sick to go anywhere."

The steroids did the trick, though, and by Tuesday I had made an obvious turnaround. I hadn't seen Sonny in a week, and for the first time I felt like missing him. Several folks tried to arrange for Sonny to come visit me, but I was on third floor where the nursery was, and that complicated matters. Finally, on Tuesday evening, Sonny was allowed to meet me in the enclosed space between the two front entrances.

Two orderlies lifted me from the bed to my chair. I had not sat up since I arrived at the hospital, and I felt strangely light-headed. Wanda and some of my friends wheeled me and my IV pole downstairs. When Mama and Daddy walked in with Sonny, he turned his head away from me. Maybe he was upset with me for having left him, maybe he didn't like seeing me hooked up to all that paraphernalia. In any case, he lay down in front of my chair and didn't move. I talked to him and told him I would be home soon. In only a few minutes, though, I grew tired of sitting up, so Mama and Daddy soon left with Sonny. I could hear him crying as we went our separate ways.

Back in my room, I was glad to lie down again. The pain had eased enough for the morphine pump to be removed, and I was soon free of the IV. Emmy spent the night with me. Surprisingly enough, I went home the next day. As Emmy was loading the van with my vast array of flowers, someone asked if she was from the florist shop!

I could sit up for only a short time, so a hospital bed was set up in the living room. I wrestled with it for a night, then sent it back and decided in favor of the sofa during the day and my bed at night. The massive doses of steroids now kept me from sleeping. I would lie awake for hours on end, finally falling asleep from sheer exhaustion, only to awaken thirty minutes later. I watched enough episodes of Andy Griffith to last a lifetime.

Homer and Ouida arrived on Friday night. Homer sat down on my bed and said, "Baby, can I do anything for you?" I held out my hand and smiled weakly. "Just sit here and talk to me," I said. It felt good just to have him near. They left on Sunday morning during one of my brief spurts of sleep.

Back in the medical arena, a dye test performed at the local hospital indicated that no medicine was flowing through the pump's catheter. And the oral medicine wasn't powerful enough to help. The doctor who managed the medicine in my pump was several hours away. But he wanted to perform the dye test himself. The problem was that I could sit up for only a few minutes at a time before the wrenching pain set in. Mama solved the problem by buying an air mattress so I could lie down on the floor of the van.

When we were ready to make the long trek, my cousin Phil, Shirley, and my friend Wanda eased me into the van, propped a pillow under my hurting leg, and covered me with a sheet. Phil drove, and Shirley sat with me on the floor of the van. I was able to eat tiny bites of a corn dog for lunch.

When we arrived at the doctor's office, his assistant had set aside a room for me with a recliner in it. He helped Phil move me from my chair into the recliner to wait until the doctor was ready for me.

The doctor injected dye into my pump and watched it move through the catheter. The dye was blocked before it reached my spine. Confirmed – the catheter was broken. It had to be repaired. I was sent home to wait until surgery could be arranged. I discovered the hard way that when something goes awry after surgery, no other surgeon will touch the case.

Hours blended into days, days into weeks, as I lay on the sofa and watched the summer go by outside the glass panes of my kitchen door. I was so weak that chewing was difficult. Mama and Daddy dreamed up every kind of food that might "work," even watermelon juice. Lisa told Mama that eggs were a high quality nutrient; and since they were easy to chew, I had eggs in every shape, form, and fashion.

We had round-the-clock help; Wanda was in and out while she worked; and friends came to visit. Still, the hours dragged by. I wasn't used to this kind of confinement.

Finally, I got an appointment with the surgeon for Monday, August 22nd – 19 days after I had come home from the hospital. Once more, I made the long trek lying on the floor of the van.

The doctor wanted to operate on Wednesday, but I pleaded with him not to send me home. He agreed and scheduled surgery for the next day.

We left the doctor's office and drove into the hospital parking lot. It was strangely familiar – the same place I'd had the first surgery nine months before. I had the same pre-op workup as before. Then an orderly wheeled me to my room and helped me into bed. Shirley was staying with me. Phil had to leave. He said, "You'll be fine. I'll be back to get you soon." Tears rolled down my cheeks. I didn't want to be here, but I had no choice.

Mama and Wanda came the next day. They got to the hospital just in time to see me before I went into the operating room.

I awoke in recovery. My back was hurting from the fresh incision. I saw the doctor sitting across the room. "My back hurts," I told him.

"Yeah, it's gonna hurt," he said.

I wanted to scream out, "I know that, but can't you give me something?"

Back in my room, the orderlies used a sheet to slide me from the gurney onto the bed, scraping my newly cut back. "Could you just lift her onto the bed?" Shirley asked as she saw the painful expression on my face.

"No," came the reply. "We don't do it that way." I couldn't think of a better time to start.

When the surgeon made his post-op rounds, he explained that the catheter had sheared (broken) in half and that he had been able to remove only one of the halves. "Why did it break?" I wanted to know. He explained that the spasticity in my back had, over the nine-month period, cut the tubing in half. "Could it happen again?" I asked.

"Yes," he replied, "but this time I put the catheter to the side of your spine, so it should be less likely to break." Still, the very thought that this whole ordeal could be replayed at any time left me almost panic-stricken.

I stayed in the hospital three nights. Wanda and Mama relieved Shirley;

then Emmy came to relieve Mama and Wanda. I was worried that I wouldn't be able to sit up for the ride home – and this time I had to sit up. I would have to stop at the pain clinic to have my pump filled before I came home, and my back couldn't handle being lifted into and out of the van that many times.

Wanda helped me try sitting up before she left, but I quickly said, "Lay me back down." Then, on Emmy's watch, I asked her to help me sit up in bed. She watched my face carefully for signs of distress. I smiled. "It's okay," I said. "I can handle it." We practiced twice more and decided that I could indeed ride home sitting in my chair.

Phil came the next day with the van to bring me home, just as he had promised. As Phil, Emmy and I traveled along, Emmy's cell phone rang. It was Lisa. We four cousins, more like brother and sisters, rejoiced that at last I was on the road to recovery.

My recovery, though, was painfully slow. I was dreadfully weak, both physically and emotionally. I was confused about why I had been taken to the very brink of death, only to be brought back – back to a body that was less healthy, less functional, more pain-ridden than it had ever been.

My weak and helpless state conjured up fears of having to return to a long brick building. I had long talks with Pastor Rusty as I poured out to him my painful childhood experiences and my fears of going through such torment again. Rusty listened intently, finally commenting, "I have always been curious about what was behind your incredible steel will, and now I have a better idea of why you refuse to give in to your condition." As he empathized with me, he also did much to assuage my fears and to reassure me that the days of the long brick building were over forever.

I went back to work two weeks after my surgery – the Tuesday after Labor Day. I had been away for seven weeks, and I felt like a ghost coming back. Everyone greeted me with hugs and looks of immense relief – and some degree of surprise – to see me again. It felt good to be wrapped so warmly in arms that I had missed so much.

One distinct memory I have, though, is of driving my chair down the hall at work and musing to myself, "I don't think I'm supposed to be here. I'm supposed to be in heaven." But God had not called me home – not yet – and I had to figure out why I was still here. I certainly was of no physical help to anyone; in fact, I needed an enormous amount of care myself. I fought hard to overcome the idea that I was too much of a burden. God still wanted me here for a reason all His own. It wasn't my job to second guess Him – to say, "Are you sure?" It was my job to say, "Yes, Lord, your will be done." Only He could decide how long my race would be; it was my task to run it all the way to the finish line.

I was tired, though. I didn't really want to run any more. Even as I write these words, though, I'm looking at a framed picture of an eagle on the wall in my office. On each side of the eagle are the words, "But they that wait upon the Lord shall renew their strength; they shall mount up with wings as eagles; they shall run and not be weary; and they shall walk and not faint." (Isaiah 40:31) I have faith that God will continue to renew my strength, day by day, until I've finished the work He has for me to do. Then I can, with a glad heart, walk (yes, walk) hand-in-hand with Him into that land where there will be no more pain, only perfect joy.

Angel in the Night

The days and nights I spent in the hospital after the catheter in my spine broke are mostly a blur. Suddenly cut off from the medicine that had been pumped through that catheter, I went into the worst withdrawal imaginable. The pain was too intense even for morphine. I would sleep for a few minutes; then the pain would break through and I'd beg for someone to push the morphine button again. I was too weak to say much more than "Help," but everyone who stayed with me recognized the look on my face that meant the pain was more than I could bear.

The room was dark that night – that night Patsy came. She knocked quietly on the door and came in. My face was grimaced, my legs contorted from the spasms that wracked my body. She smiled and said, "Are you having a hard time, baby girl?" It was more an acknowledgment than a question. She said, "I'm staying with you tonight." I made a weak protest, reminding her that she had to work the next day. But in my heart I wanted her to stay.

Patsy's coming was an unexpected answer to an unvoiced prayer that I not be left with strangers. Patsy was far from being a stranger. We had gone to elementary and high school together, and Patsy had been a special friend all those years. She had pushed my wheelchair down many a hall and walkway and had sat beside me in class and helped me take notes and turn pages. Best of all, though, we had talked together and laughed together, the way friends do.

In adulthood Patsy and I saw each other less often. We each had a career, and Patsy had a husband and children who kept her busy. Still, there were those special times when we saw each other, and we knew our friendship had never changed. That night in the hospital was one of those times. My voice was weak and barely comprehensible; nevertheless, I felt safe with Patsy.

The pain never actually subsided that night, but for some reason it was slightly less intense if I dangled my legs off the side of the bed. So I lay in that position most of the night – crossways on the bed. Patsy lay next to me and rubbed my legs gently, being careful not to move them. The morphine pump was programmed to deliver a few drops every five minutes; yet I begged Patsy to push the button far more often. She always obliged and smilingly gave me a "thumbs up" when the machine sounded a successful beep. When the pain grew unbearably fierce, whimpers escaped my throat and tears rolled down my cheeks. I didn't weep alone, though. Patsy wept, too, assuring me, "I'm right here, my little baby girl."

During the moments when the morphine had taken some of the edge off the pain, Patsy was able to make me laugh. A nurse brought in a diaper for me, and Patsy spread it out wide and laughed heartily, wondering how to fit my tiny bottom into an apparatus that must have been made for a man three times my size. Later my linens had to be changed, and a nurse bent on doing things her own way was trying to move my legs even though I begged her not to. Patsy intervened and informed the nurse that we didn't need her help. When the nurse left, Patsy mused, "I thought I was just going to have to throw her out that window." Her gestures made me laugh.

Patsy stayed the entire night, with never a thought of leaving me until someone came to relieve her the next morning. She offered to stay again, but family members from distant places began arriving to help. Even so, Patsy still came every evening after work to see me. She didn't stop when I left the hospital either. Every day shortly after 5:00 her car would pull into my driveway, and she'd come in and sit with me and hold my hand and smile at me as I lay on the sofa. I watched the clock and waited for her to come. Her visits were a bright spot in long days filled with pain and uncertainty.

I believe in angels. God sent one that night to take care of His child.

Teaching "Introduction to Special Education"

The idea came to me as I was recovering from the ordeal with the infamous pump. Not knowing how long this one would last and not knowing the outcome if it were to break again, I had a deep desire to make a difference in the lives of future teachers and the children they would have under their care. I was already teaching an online course in "Introduction to Special Education," and I was able to share some of my experiences with the students through that course. But it was nothing like seeing the students face-to-face and sharing my story with them.

I went to the Dean and explained my wish to have an opportunity to teach in a live classroom. He arranged for me to co-teach with another instructor the following semester. A year later, I began teaching a class on my own. My teaching opportunities proved to be a huge success, with students being exposed to a disability considered severe, not to mention lifelong. I shared with them my experience of being denied access to public education, explaining that experiences such as mine paved the way for the legislation that now protects the educational rights of all children with disabilities.

For my online class, with the help of the media department at Ole Miss, I produced a video that introduced me to the class. I typically put this video online about halfway through the semester so that the students would have gotten accustomed to the idea that I was a "normal" professor. Then, when they saw the video, I wanted them to be surprised – to discover that looks can be deceiving. If they had seen the video earlier, they might have stereotyped me as a "different" professor. I enjoyed reading their comments about the video and finding how their perspectives had changed.

These are excerpts from some of the comments I received:

Let me begin by saying it was such as pleasant surprise to finally get to meet you. I was so impressed with your positive attitude considering the obvious obstacles you've had to overcome. You certainly have proven that students with physical impairments/disabilities can be all that they choose to be. I admire your determination in seeking the education you deserved. You had the choice to sit back and do nothing or get things moving. You were undoubtedly more than this world was ready for in the 1960's; good for you! I must say, not only am I impressed with your education credentials, but I am extremely proud to be one of your students. While reading each week in the text, my thoughts repeatedly agree that students with disabilities have every right to a fair and appropriate education; however, it wasn't until after your interview that I recognized just how profound that statement really proves to be. Your video helps me to realize that as an educator I may be unable to resolve the difficulties my students may encounter. But that is okay. What I can do is enhance their self-esteem, teach them to respect one another's differences, give them the opportunity to learn, and provide the encouragement for them to succeed. You are an amazing lady who has accomplished so much more than many of us. I commend your bravery and persistence. Your video touched me greatly, and I want to extend my sincere appreciation to you for sharing your story with me.

Dr. Harper, your story and video have really made me realize that just because you have a disability does not mean you cannot have big dreams and accomplish those dreams. Dr. Harper is an inspiration to everyone. You had people in your life that really helped and believed in you. They always say that the people you are around can really affect you. I knew just by reading your responses to my work that you were a very remarkable woman. You are remembered not because of your disability but because of your strong words. I just hope that I can be the great teacher you are one day. You are an inspiration to everyone. I'm glad you shared your story and video with me.

Teaching the live class has been especially unique. On the first day of class, it's obvious that the students are wondering what on earth is going on here. They have some difficulty understanding my speech at first, but soon it becomes second nature to them. The most interesting occurrence is that my class becomes similar to a small community in which the students become close and are willing to share with the rest of the class some of their own struggles. When I discuss my early experiences at the long brick building (which I refer to as the "hell hole"), many of the students become outraged. It's apparent that this may be the first time that some of them have had a chance to develop strong feelings about a social issue. One day in class I was telling of an incident that occurred in the "hell hole"; and one of my big strapping boys stood straight up and said in a gruff voice, "Where are those people?"

My students seem to especially benefit from the "awareness" activities we do. "Get out your cell phones," I tell them (of course, they all have one). "Now, put your hands in a fist, dial the phone and hold it up to your ear." After fumbling with the phone for a couple of minutes, the students say, "Wow! I can't do that." They realize how challenged I am by the simplest things they do all the time. But then I show them some of the devices that do make my life easier, like my special keyboard and mouse and my word prediction software. I even let them drive my power chair (on very low speed), and they discover that it's harder to drive than it appears.

I think what surprises the students most is that the "city" of cerebral palsy is not where I would have chosen to live. I share with them a piece written by the mother of a child with Down Syndrome. She compares having a child with a disability to taking a trip to Holland when she had imagined going to Italy.

WELCOME TO HOLLAND
by Emily Perl Kingsley
© 1987 by Emily Perl Kingsley. All rights reserved.
Reprinted by permission of the author

I am often asked to describe the experience of raising a child with a disability - to try to help people who have not shared that unique experience to understand it, to imagine how it would feel. It's like this......

When you're going to have a baby, it's like planning a fabulous vacation trip - to Italy. You buy a bunch of guide books and make your wonderful plans. The Coliseum. The Michelangelo David. The gondolas in Venice. You may learn some handy phrases in Italian. It's all very exciting.

After months of eager anticipation, the day finally arrives. You pack your bags and off you go. Several hours later, the plane lands. The flight attendant comes in and says, "Welcome to Holland."

"Holland?!?" you say. "What do you mean Holland?? I signed up for Italy! I'm supposed to be in Italy. All my life I've dreamed of going to Italy."
But there's been a change in the flight plan. They've landed in Holland and there you must stay.

The important thing is that they haven't taken you to a horrible, disgusting, filthy place, full of pestilence, famine and disease. It's just a different place.
So you must go out and buy new guide books. And you must learn a whole new language. And you will meet a whole new group of people you would never have met.

It's just a different place. It's slower-paced than Italy, less flashy than Italy. But after you've been there for a while and you catch your breath, you look around.... and you begin to notice that Holland has windmills....and Holland has tulips.

Holland even has Rembrandts.

But everyone you know is busy coming and going from Italy... and they're all bragging about what a wonderful time they had there. And for the rest of your life, you will say "Yes, that's where I was supposed to go. That's what I had planned." And the pain of that will never, ever, ever, ever go away... because the loss of that dream is a very, very significant loss.

But... if you spend your life mourning the fact that you didn't get to Italy, you may never be free to enjoy the very special, the very lovely things ... about Holland.

The idea of living one's life in a different place than what one might prefer made such an impression on one of my students that she wrote the following paper about a child in her class. I think Diane had already caught a glimpse of the light I tried to show my students; but when I read this paper, I knew she had captured the light in all its brilliance.

Diane
Student Teacher

Through the Eyes of a Child

I was honored to have a teacher who took me to Holland when I wanted to see Paris. Physically, I have not visited either location; mentally, I have. Helen Keller once said 'the best and most beautiful things in the world...must be felt within the heart.' Dr. Harper showed my EDSP 308 class how to look with our hearts. I have not seen Holland or Paris, but I have felt them through the eyes of a child.

I met K.S the first day of student teaching. He nearly ran over me with his power wheelchair. I asked him if he had a license to drive his vehicle. His laughter, long eyelashes, and dark brown hair melted my heart. I must admit I did look at his disabilities for a moment. His personal sidekick, his nurse, informed me K.S has never walked. His wheelchair is equipped with a suction machine, tubes attached to a ventilator and his tracheotomy, and a horn that he purposely forgets to use.

K.S can read on a first grade level, although he reads with the aid of a magnifying glass. Sometimes he likes to read with the book at eye level, literally. K.S reads with the book approximately two inches from his face. He is a whiz at math facts. While others are counting on their fingers, K.S is asking the class to inform him when they are finished. Math facts are in his head, not on his fingers, he informed me.

One day I wanted the students to earn hot chocolate as a reward for good behavior. I asked the students to write a paragraph about hot chocolate. How did it taste? When is your favorite time to drink hot chocolate? I did not take into consideration K.S is tube fed. His paragraph spoke to my heart.

"Hot chocolate is brown. It is hot and could burn my skin. Some people drink it when it is real cold outside. I do not know what hot chocolate tastes like. I can only wonder what it tastes like."

The students earned hot chocolate for good behavior one month later. All the students were enjoying a cup of hot chocolate while listening to a story on tape. I noticed K.S with his wheelchair turned towards the door. He wanted to leave the classroom while the other students drank their hot chocolate. I walked over to K.S and asked his nurse if he could try some hot chocolate. She informed me that K.S could have a small taste, if he wanted to try.

"Hey, speed racer! Would you like some hot chocolate?"

"Yes, ma'am!!!"

I felt as if my plane landed in Paris. K.S continued to show me Paris everyday at school. He and I had lunch one day. He experienced the taste of a cheese stick. The smile on his face was all I needed to see. He and I played dinosaurs on his wheelchair tray and we exchanged hugs at the end of the school day. He read and helped write lines for the play in class about trees. He played the part of the 'protector of the tree.' I wish I could have stayed in Paris.

One day he asked if I would like to sign his book.

"K.S., I did not know you wrote a book. I would be honored to sign your book."

"Mrs. T., I did not write a book. My book is for my friends to sign. You are my friend."

It is difficult for me to leave Paris. I experienced Paris through the eyes of a child. K.S took me to the most beautiful sights and sounds. Helen Keller was right about the 'beautiful things in the world.' They are felt within your heart.

My Cheerleader

Everybody should have one – a cheerleader – someone who sees the best in us, someone who makes us know we're loved, someone who picks us up when we're down, someone who shares our successes with praises lofty enough for a Nobel Prize Winner. A cheerleader makes us believe in ourselves even when circumstances are tossing winds of discouragement our way.

I'm lucky – I've had a very special cheerleader since I was in 9th grade. Her name is Mrs. Smith – Patsy Smith. She taught me Mississippi History and Civics, and she was a master teacher of those subjects. But actually she taught me much more than that. Every day when I wheeled into her classroom, a profound sense of happiness and security swept over me. Her wide smile, her gentle pat on the back, her words of praise and encouragement helped me make it through those tough adolescent years when being different is the worst plague anyone could have. She helped me remember that my broken body wasn't who I was.

Little did I realize that Mrs. Smith was watching in agony as I typed one keystroke after another until my hair was drenched with perspiration. Much later she confided in me that my struggles to complete the written work in her class had troubled her so much that she went to see the principal to ask how she could make it easier for me. Mr. Davis, wise man that he was, said, "She doesn't want to be treated any differently. She wants to make it on her own." So Mrs. Smith gave me no concessions, no special treatment. But she couldn't quite resist letting her pride in me show. And that made all the difference.

At some point Mrs. Smith blended friend with teacher and became Patsy. She followed me through high school and college, sharing each milestone with me. When she moved to Arkansas and began working at a community college, she continued to motivate students to become all they could be. She created a "Maxine" wall in her office, where she hung newspaper clippings about my achievements, including my earning a doctorate degree. She told me how students would come into her office ready to give up and how she would take them to her "Yes, you can" wall. There she showed them that their obstacles were minute compared to mine, and there she helped them see that "Yes, you can" achieve your dreams.

When my book *Daffodils in the Snow* came into print, Patsy became my most enthusiastic promoter. She arranged for me to come to Blytheville, where she lived, and do a book signing at That Bookstore. She later wrote me this e-mail:

"*Congratulations, Miss Best Selling Author!!! Connie at That Bookstore told me yesterday your book was the BEST SELLING MOTHER'S DAY BOOK, OUTSELLING BILLY GRAHAM!!!!! What do you think about that?!? They are thrilled and people are even giving them for graduation gifts. Not only that, but Joyce King who attended your book signing taught my mother's Sunday School class last week and used your book. She said you have made a place in her heart and you would never leave it. Every time she reads your book she gets even more out of it. She said just meeting you and your mother and sister was a blessing in her life and that she felt sure you might "have her moments but that Dr. Maxine Harper had to be the closest to a saint" she has ever been around and that "she probably is a saint. If you want to see God's love and joy just look in Maxine's face. And it comes through in this incredible book!" You will never fully know how God is using you to be His inspiration here on earth. Dear Maxine, you have transcended mere mortals by your wonderful witness. What a blessing you are to so, so, so many people you have never even met!!"*

Patsy faithfully reminded me that I was of value to her and to those with whom I came into contact, either in person or through Daffodils. She bought endless copies of Daffodils and gave them to friends who needed encouragement. She never failed to tell me when the book had a special impact on its recipient. I think Patsy somehow knew that such stories nourished my heart. One Christmas Patsy sent me a place setting of daffodil flatware. How I cherish it as a reminder that she carries my flame of hope right along with me!

Time marched on, and Patsy and I each had life experiences, good and bad, that we shared with each other. One day in April 1996, I opened a letter from Patsy. As I read it, tears streamed down my face. Patsy's daughter-in-law and 3-month-old granddaughter had been hit by a drunk driver. Patsy's daughter-in-law died at the scene. The baby died two days later in Patsy's arms. I remember her writing that her arms would forever ache from the void left by that precious baby girl. My shock was so great that I don't remember what I wrote in return except that I shared her grief as much as a friend possibly can.

Patsy and I have developed an incredible sixth sense about knowing when each other needs encouragement. On April 25, 2000, I sent Patsy an e-mail saying, "Patsy, when I read this, I thought of you -- my cheerleader who always saw something of value in me."

Attached to the e-mail was a story about a cracked pot. The cracked pot was able to deliver to the master's house only half the water delivered by the perfect pot. The cracked pot felt ashamed – that is, until the water bearer showed him the beautiful flowers that grew on his side of the path. The story continued as the bearer said to the cracked pot, "Did you notice that there were flowers only on your side of your path, but not on the other pot's side? That's because I have always known about your flaw, and I took advantage of it. I planted flower seeds on your side of the path, and every day while we walk back from the stream, you've watered them. For two years I have been able to pick these beautiful flowers to decorate my master's table. Without your being just the way you are, he would not have this beauty to grace his house."

The story continued, "Each of us has our own unique flaws. We're all cracked pots. But if we will allow it, the Lord will use our flaws to grace His Father's table. In God's great economy, nothing goes to waste. So as we seek ways to minister together, and as God calls you to the tasks He has appointed for you, don't be afraid of your flaws. Acknowledge them, and allow Him to take advantage of them, and you, too, can be the cause of beauty in His pathway. Go out boldly, knowing that in our weakness we find His strength, and that 'In Him every one of God's promises is a Yes.'"

Patsy replied immediately:

Maxine.....How did you know I needed your precious words tonite?!? Four years ago today our precious little Mary Witten died two days after her cherished mother....all because a 42 year old woman CHOSE to drink and drive. It seems forever since I have held her because I have missed them forever it seems...yet it seems like the heartache began just a moment ago at times the pain is so raw. Then you, my precious Friend, reach out to me saying, "Go out boldly, knowing that in our weakness we find His strength," and that "In Him every one of God's promises is a Yes."

If we can only remember everything is in God's time...our answers, our reunions, our eternal joys...all of the YESes to come. What peace this gives me!

Patsy continued to cheer me on, no matter the circumstances. When I became critically ill in July 2005, Patsy again rallied her prayer warriors on my behalf, as she had done so many times before. It wasn't the season for daffodils, but to my hospital room came the largest bouquet of yellow flowers I had ever seen. There must have been every variety of yellow flower that the florist could get her hands on. Though death knocked at my door, it didn't come in. I went home from the hospital on August 3rd, the date of this e-mail from Patsy:

Please know you are SO close in my heart and prayers. I just have to tell you yet one more time (how MANY does this make?!?!) how you enrich my life in so many ways. You are our encourager, our inspiration, our motivator, our HERO!!! How God blessed my life gifting me with you as one of my students! That blessing

mulitiplied into sooooo many more through the years, and I am grateful!
The blessing is mine to have such a cheerleader as Patsy, and I am grateful.

Granny

"Thimble, thimble, who's got the thimble?" Granny would chime as she held out her two closed hands and asked us to guess which had the thimble. That was one of the many games she played with her grandchildren when we were little. Granny, Daddy's mother, lived in the country with her daughter and son-in-law. When I was young, away at the long brick building, I saw Granny only during my quarterly vacations at home. So my early memories of her are sparse.

I do remember that Granny always had snow white hair that she wore up in a bun, usually covered by a knit cap to keep out drafts. Let down, Granny's hair was long, reaching below her waist. As children, we liked to watch her comb it. The ends were reddish-blond, like the color of her hair when she was young.

Granny liked to sew by hand. She made each of her eleven grandchildren a quilt top from fabric that she had used to make her own dresses.

Of Norwegian descent, Granny had a name that reflected her heritage – Mary Corinna Flanagin. Her ancestors had an interesting entry into the United States. Granny's grandfather Christopherson was a ship's carpenter and was working on a ship in India when an epidemic of cholera broke out. He decided to take the next ship out to try to escape the epidemic. Finding a ship destined for America, he seized the opportunity and came to the states. He never returned to Norway, but soon sent for his family, who joined him in this country around 1867. As the story goes, they were in the Chicago area when the father met someone who was visiting from Carroll County, Mississippi, and told him of the need for carpenters in Mississippi. (This was during the period of Reconstruction following the Civil War). So he moved to Mississippi with his family.

Granny's grandfather built several pieces of furniture that they brought with them on the ship. One piece contained drawers in which they stored hardtack, a type of bread that wouldn't spoil. Granny told of her grandmother making and storing a large amount of hardtack for the long voyage across the Atlantic. She had enough to provide not only for her own children but for others on the voyage as well.

Before she married, Granny was a school teacher. She was one of the few women of her day who had attended college. Granny taught in a one-room schoolhouse, and two of her students were her twin brothers. The story goes that one day her father passed by the school in his wagon. The two little boys saw their Papa riding by and ran out to the wagon. Papa scooped up the little fellows, set them beside him on the seat, and rode off. Their sister/teacher could only smile.

Granny married Hiram Matthew ("Mac") Harper, a farmer, and they raised a family of three boys and one girl. Those were Depression times, so they grew their own vegetables, milked their own cows, caught their own fish, and hung their own beef and pork to dry. They bought only flour, sugar, and salt.

Although Granny stopped teaching to raise her family, she instilled in each of her children – and grandchildren – the value of an education. All four children graduated from high school, and two went on to graduate from college. Two of her sons served in World War II, and the other became a minister. Four of her grandchildren became teachers.

Granny's husband died of cancer in the 1940's, when she was only in her fifties. She lived about 40 more years, dying in 1981 at age 94.

From Granny's four children came 11 grandchildren – seven girls and four boys – and, at last count, 17 great grandchildren and 9 great-great grandchildren. She lived to see all 11 grandchildren and 4 great grandchildren.

Granny left her house only to go to church – our little family church down the road from her house – and to go to her family doctor in town. Even though her physical world was limited, her mental world was broad. She kept up with world affairs by listening to the radio and reading the newspaper.

In her last years Granny was bedridden. Her bedroom was small, allowing only two or three visitors at one time. I think she may have liked it that way, so she could enjoy each person individually.

I remember squeezing my chair through the door of her bedroom and sitting with her as she shared her faith, her knowledge, and her insight with me. I wish I had been wise enough to take notes! Myself 27 when Granny died, I was old enough to have gained some knowledge but not yet old enough to realize that it takes more than knowledge to produce the wisdom of years.

The Harper Cousins

At a dinner meeting one evening, I was shocked to hear someone say, "I have first cousins I haven't even met." I immediately piped up, "Well, my first cousins are like brothers and sisters to me." And so they are.

I'm the sixth of eleven Harper grandchildren – four boys and seven girls. We represent four Harper children – my Daddy (Uncle Maxie), Aunt Elma, Uncle Moss, and Uncle Macey. I must say that God did a mighty fine thing for me when He plopped me down in the middle of this family. As you will see, each one is precious to me in his or her own way, and together they have brought a richness to my life that defies words.

Lisa, exactly six months between Wanda and me in age, is the oldest daughter of Uncle Macey and Laura Lee. Living only a few blocks from our house, Lisa was our childhood playmate. We rode in the golf cart together, went to the lake together, and spent lots of Friday nights together. Lisa, Wanda, and I were in the same grade from sixth grade through high school. Along with Wanda and many others, Lisa was one of those dear friends who rolled my wheelchair and typewriter from one class to the next. We commuted to college together in my van one summer – the summer Lisa learned to drive a stick shift.

After college and medical school, Lisa did her internship in Dallas. While visiting her there one summer, we went to Six Flags. I was hesitant to ride the scary rides that Lisa liked. There was one ride in particular that Lisa insisted on riding – a roller coaster of sorts with sharp turns and dips. The problem was that lots of other people wanted to ride it, too. Lisa decided to capitalize on my wheelchair to get us to the front of the line. When I resisted, Lisa cajoled me, "Oh, it's a baby ride." So I agreed and got on. I smelled a rat when the attendant buckled me in tightly. Just before we zoomed off, Lisa looked back at me and grinned as she said, "I lied."

As the years rolled on, I called Lisa many times for advice, sometimes medical, sometimes just sisterly. Today we live miles apart, but we're never very far away in heart. Lisa came to be with me when the catheter to my baclofen pump broke and I became deathly ill. She came just because – just because she loved me and I needed her.

Lauri Anne, Lisa's sister, is three years younger than I. Tall, strong, and fun-loving, she gave me adventures. We became close friends when I was in college and Lauri Anne was still in high school. My mother had to have surgery, and Lauri Anne took turns with another friend staying with me at night. Lauri Anne and I talked late into the night – which was great fun except that we had to get up at 5:00 in the morning so I could be ready to leave with my carpool at 6:30. Poor Lauri Anne! She was not a morning person, and I'm not sure she had ever seen 5:00 a.m. Despite those early mornings, our friendship grew and flourished.

Lauri Anne spent her freshman year in college at the same school I was attending. One night she wanted me to visit her in the dorm – a feat that was trickier than it sounds. She lived on the third floor of a very old dorm with no elevator, so she picked me up and carried me up three flights of stairs. That was the first of many "adventures" with Lauri Anne. She took me on my first and only escalator ride as the people looking down on us gasped! She took me to the beach, where we discovered that wheelchairs sink in sand. Never fear, Lauri Anne took me out of the chair, dug a hole in the sand, and set me in it so I could enjoy the beach.

The years passed. Lauri Anne took a teaching job in Louisiana, got married, and began a family of five children. When Wanda became pregnant with Avent, we were sworn to secrecy until Travis's mother had been told. I had to tell someone, though, and that someone was Lauri Anne. I said excitedly, "Wanda's pregnant." Lauri Anne laughed and said, "So am I!" Lauri Anne's second child, Greg, was born two weeks after Avent.

Today Lauri Anne and I live miles apart, but we're never very far away in heart. Lauri Anne came to be with me when the catheter to my baclofen pump broke and I became deathly ill. She came just because – just because she loved me and I needed her. Have you read those words before?

Emmy, my youngest cousin, is Lisa's and Lauri Anne's sister. In college Emmy played the best "Eliza Doolittle" I've ever seen. After college, Emmy married, moved to Colorado, and became an attorney. For many years we saw her only during holidays. Oh, what we were missing! Emmy and Ray finally moved to Alabama, and we saw them more often, but still not often enough. At last they moved back to Mississippi, and we grew ever closer to them. Emmy now has her own room at my house. She and my Daddy have a running joke about car keys. One day she picked up the wrong keys and came back to get the right ones. My Daddy teased, "Oh, go ahead and take those," to which Emmy replied, "Well, I happen to be picky about my keys!"

After moving back to Mississippi, Emmy had to take the bar exam again to be licensed in this state. It was during the time while Emmy wasn't working that I had my first baclofen pump implant surgery. She came to the rescue and took turns with my mother spending the first few days with me in the hospital. Always the comedian, Emmy likes to tell how, after I was taken from the "holding room" to the operating room, she had doctors, nurses, everyone running for cover as she drove my power chair down the long halls and back to my room.

Nine months later, Emmy was with me in New Orleans when I found out that the pump's catheter had to be replaced. She came back a week later when I went into full withdrawal and nearly lost my life. When I had surgery again to replace the broken catheter, Emmy came to help. I tease her even now, "You didn't have time for a job. You were too busy helping me!" In reality, we both believe that God chose her especially for times such as these.

Emmy does have a job now, but she hasn't given up her job of looking after me, as well as my folks. Emmy is always there when we need her – just because – just because she loves us.

Marty is the oldest of Uncle Macey's and Laura Lee's children – the big brother of Lisa, Lauri Anne, and Emmy. Marty was accepted into the Air Force Academy immediately after graduating from high school. In the Air Force he did a stint in Florida, then attended Duke University in North Carolina. While in North Carolina, he met and married Charlotte. Marty later did stints in Alaska, St. Louis, and England before settling in San Antonio. A few years ago he retired from the Air Force with the rank of Colonel. He comes back to his Carroll County land as often as he can.

Marty loves to pick on his girl relatives. Once when he was here, he teased me about my $1 plates that were copies of my good china. "I can tell the difference. See," he said, holding up one of the inexpensive plates, "this one says 'China' on the back, so it must be the real thing."

This is a typical e-mail from Marty, written prior to a Thanksgiving when about 15 strong came to visit:

For your planning purposes the boys (Adam, Chris, Greg, Taylor, etc) like to pile into one room or utility closet and sleep in sleeping bags or the like. I think sleeping under the porch with the dogs would be fun for them also. They would also like a wide screen TV and catered meals 4 times a day if that is not too much trouble.

The young ladies have also often crashed in one bedroom (although Patty is certainly becoming more high maintenance and may require a private bath and would love a hot tub).

Hope that helps. Flexibility is the key to Airpower; No plan survives first contact with the enemy.

Mary Esther, daughter of Aunt Elma and Uncle Willard, was the first born of the cousins. She and I became really close when I reached adulthood. Mary Esther lives in Carroll County and attends our little church, so I've been seeing her every Sunday for a long, long time. We also began traveling together, including three trips to DisneyWorld. The weather wasn't cooperative on our last trip, and we still laugh at the thought of ourselves in a sea of yellow ponchos with black headbands over our ears. Our motto was, "We don't care how we look because we're cold and wet; and besides, we'll never see these people again."

Mary Esther also went with friends Homer and Ouida and me to Branson, where we laughed about our $30 hot dog meal and our tour guide – the lady with the pink feathery sweater, whom we appropriately nicknamed "Miss Pinky."

Whenever we're together, Mary Esther has an uncanny knack for knowing what I need even before I ask. On one trip, I had a sudden breakthrough of pain. Mary Esther took one look at my face and said, "You need some medicine, don't you?"

I'll always remember the tender care Mary Esther took of her parents. When leukemia began to wrack Aunt Elma's frail body, Mary Esther was always there for her. Staying in the hospital for days at a time and reading the same magazines again and again, Mary Esther laid down her magazine one afternoon and laughingly said, "Well, Mama, I'm ready for my test. What about you?" Forever etched in my memory, though, is the sight of Aunt Elma in her last days using a walker to make her painful way from the kitchen to her bedroom, and Mary Esther walking ever so slowly behind her mother to keep her from falling.

Mary Esther is now grandmother to two young boys whose antics she loves to share.

Mary Esther's brother, Mac, is the craftsman in the family. Everyone loves his nativity scenes carved from wood. Hanging in my house I also have a picture of an angel and a picture of the Last Supper, both wood carvings made by Mac.

Mac and Judy are now grandparents, too. When their son Tim told his little boy Hunter that he was going to have a brother or sister, the tyke replied, "Well, I want two brothers and three sisters." Tim quickly shook his head and said, "Hey, wait a minute – we're not taking orders."

Uncle Moss and Aunt Violet were parents to Ben, Jane, and Phil. Ben has a dry wit that keeps us all laughing. His career as a high school teacher and assistant principal provided plenty of fodder for his stories. My favorite was about "the Chinese fire drill," as he called it. To recount, the curtains in the auditorium caught on fire one day, and the fire alarm sounded. Someone in the office thought the alarm was sounding by mistake and shut it off, whereupon someone from the auditorium sent word to turn the alarm on again. By this time, children and adults were running in all directions with no clue as to whether there actually was a fire. Thus ensued "the Chinese fire drill."

Another of Ben's stories is about an automobile accident in which his wife Arma was involved. Arma happened to be on the way to the beauty shop, and nothing would deter her from an appointment with her beautician. When the policeman offered to drive her home or to the hospital, Arma had another idea. According to Ben's commentary, the policeman radioed headquarters with the message, "En route with accident victim to Nouveau Hair."

Ben's comic side is sweetly balanced by a tender side that truly appreciates family. On the Easter Sunday when we dedicated the annex to our small family church, I asked Ben to conduct the service. He had a beautiful delivery, warm and gracious and very stately. He surprised me by closing it with these words before the benediction: "We appreciate Maxine's organizing this service. She is a blessing to this church and to this family." The lump in my throat is still there.

Jane is the cousin we think of as sweet and demure. When we played football in the country, Jane was the one who dropped to the ground rather than be tackled. She's a meticulous housekeeper, just like her mother was. She also has a lovely singing voice and is a talented floral arranger. Jane followed in her father's footsteps and became the lay speaker at our small family church, where we put all her gifts to good use. I often notice Jane standing in the pulpit in the same way her father stood, with her hands softly folded. Her messages reflect her ability as a teacher to instruct, inspire, and encourage. She laughingly shakes her head when we say she preaches or when we refer to her message as a sermon.

Jane lives about 40 miles from me – close enough that we can do together what we do best – shop! Jane also accompanied me to Mayo Clinic to have my baclofen pump evaluated, and she went with me to Mississippi State University when I was named the College of Education Alumna of the Year 2008. She was with me just because – just because she loved me and I needed her. Have you read those words before?

Phil is the youngest of the guy cousins – only a year older than I. We think of Phil as our "brainy" cousin. He always won at Trivial Pursuit, Scrabble, and all the other "smart" games.

When I was in graduate school, Phil ran a pizza restaurant in a nearby town. One night my friend Cyndi and I drove over to see Phil and eat pizza. "Just go in," I told Cyndi, "and tell Phil that you need help getting someone out of your car. He'll know who it is." She came out laughing. He knew.

Today Phil lives close by, in Carroll County. He helps take care of me – driving me places, helping me with "guy" stuff. He gently laid me on the floor of the van and drove me to the hospital several hours away to have the broken catheter to my baclofen pump replaced. A few days later, he came back to get me, just like he promised he would. He always comes just because – just because he loves me and I need him. Have you read those words before?

One day Phil and I were discussing the special relationship we have with our cousins. Until we became adults, we didn't understand that ours is a unique blessing that not every family has. I confided to Phil that I felt especially blessed to be so cared about by every single one of my cousins. Then Phil said something especially poignant – "Remember the saying, 'He ain't heavy; he's my brother.'"

Homer

I first met Homer, or rather he met me, when I was eight or nine years old. I had just returned home from the long brick building, and it still amazed and thrilled me that a bona fide adult wanted anything to do with me. And Homer wanted a lot to do with me. He and my dad started out as business colleagues, but they soon became close friends. I don't actually remember meeting Homer; it was as though I had always known him. Almost from the beginning, he sort of adopted Wanda and me as his own children.

I was still having a difficult time trusting any adults outside my family, but somehow I had no trouble trusting Homer. Children always sense when someone loves them, and I sensed that Homer saw something in me to love. He liked to make me laugh, and he even liked to play with me. We sat at the kitchen table and played double nine dominoes by the hour; and even though he may have "intended" to let me win, he still laughs as he reminisces that I actually beat him almost every time.

We looked forward to the Sunday afternoons Homer spent at our house. Those afternoons were filled with laughter as he chased Spot with the broom and had Wanda ring the doorbell so Spot would go flying to the front door, barking all the way.

Homer moved from Greenwood several years later – first to Texas, then back to south Mississippi. He still treated Wanda and me like his own children – even coming all the way to our high school graduation.

A few years later, Homer and Ouida married, and Ouida eagerly joined our

family. I say "family" because they really are like family. Through the years, they've shared our good times as well as our hard times. They were right there on the front row beside my parents when I received my doctorate degree, and I remember how happy it made me to see them clapping as I passed by them after my hooding. They were my first overnight guests in my new house. When Homer got a new truck, he took me for a ride – just the two of us – and showed me all its neat gadgets.

Homer can always make me laugh. Once, when I had taken some medicine that thinned my hair, I had to wear a wig for a few months. Homer mentioned that I had a new hair-do, to which I replied, "Actually it's not my hair." He laughed and said, "Well, whose hair is it then?"

Homer and Ouida are always there for us. They came to the hospital when Daddy had a kidney removed, and they spent two nights near the hospital when I had the baclofen/pain pump implanted. Then, when the catheter to the pump sheared in my spine, Wanda had to break the news to Homer that I might not make it. Ouida told me later that she had heard the phone ring and had asked Homer who called. He said, "I-I-I can't talk right now." That may sound like a small incident, but it was special to me – special to know how much he cared. As soon as I came home from the hospital, Homer and Ouida came for the weekend. Homer sat down on the bed beside me and asked, almost pleadingly, "Baby, can I do anything for you?"

I held out my hand and took his. My voice was barely above a whisper. "Just sit and talk to me for a while." All I wanted was for him to be near.

Homer is the best fix-it man I've ever seen. He has "operated" on my wheelchair, my automatic door, the lever doors to my laundry room, and a host of other things. I've always thought he's best, though, at fixing my spirits when they're sagging.

Kathleen

I met Kathleen at a time in my life when I especially needed a friend. I had returned home from graduate school with my Master's degree – but no job. It was one of those lonely, frightening, in-between times, except in my case the loneliness and fear were intensified. "All my friends have jobs. What if no one ever hires me?"

Then Kathleen entered my life. She was working as a reporter/photographer for the local newspaper. I was a guest columnist writing about special education issues for the paper. Kathleen and I first met when she took my picture for the column; then we became better acquainted at a meeting of the American Association of University Women. The very next day after the meeting, I was at her house visiting with her and her family. Kathleen and her husband Jim had two children to whom they kindly let me play second mother. Ruth was about 5, very smart and articulate, and fun to talk with. Tom was about 2, with chubby little hands and a precious little-boy face. He was fascinated by the big wheels on my chair.

Kathleen and I developed an immediate bond. She was kind, intelligent, and easy to be with. She seemed to understand and empathize with my frustration over not having a job. It felt so good to have a new friend nearby. I enjoyed her company.

A few months after we met, Kathleen went to work for a grant project at a nearby university. Project Paratrain, as it was called, was designed to develop a two-year curriculum for paraprofessionals working at facilities that serve people with disabilities. Cathy, a mutual friend, was the director of the project. Cathy and Kathleen knew I would love working on such a task, so they hired me as a consultant to help develop the course material. I was thrilled to be productive at last and to have some contact with the outside world.

I began working with Cathy and Kathleen in March 1980, and I worked through much of the summer – about 3 hours a day. I knew, though, that my work with the grant was temporary, and I wondered what lay beyond. Then, in July I received the offer to teach at the Little Red School – an offer that I think Cathy prompted.

Even when Kathleen and I no longer worked together, we continued to see each other often. Ruth even spent a weekend with me when her parents were out of town. Kathleen and her family filled a void that was especially poignant at that time in my life.

Kathleen was the one who introduced me to computers. She was able to foresee how much easier they would make my life – and she was absolutely right. But neither of us knew what a tremendous impact computers would have on my career.

It was a sad time for me when Kathleen's and Jim's careers moved them to Jackson, two hours away. We kept in touch by phone, but I missed seeing Kathleen. She never really left me, though. I remember calling her in tears on more than one occasion when my dissertation was giving me fits. She would tell me how to "fix" it, and then she would always reassure me, "It'll be fine." And it was.

When I achieved homeowner status, Kathleen came to see my newly built house, and her joy for me was truly evident. I took her on a "grand tour" of the house, and we gloated together over every detail. Arriving back in the breakfast room, Kathleen beamed and said, "Let's do the tour again." That's the mark of a true friend.

Kathleen and I made career changes at about the same time. I opened my own business, and Kathleen went to work at the University of Mississippi (Ole Miss). She was soon made Director of the Center for Educational Research and Evaluation at Ole Miss. We began collaborating on different projects, and I was thrilled to be working with her again.

Finally, in the summer of 2000, Kathleen told me there was an opening in her center for an educational research analyst. She encouraged me to apply, and I was hired.

Kathleen's and my life had come full circle, and we were together again, as we were meant to be. Kathleen was a patient mentor, a diligent supervisor, and a faithful friend. That combination worked well for us because we had such strong respect for each other. Not only that, we had the same mind set, often referring to our like thinking as the "twin thing."

Kathleen has always played whatever role I needed her to play at any given time. When I needed help knowing what statistical method I should use to analyze a new set of data, Kathleen was my eager teacher. When I worried about meeting deadlines, Kathleen was my competent leader. But then there was the day in her office when I thought my pump had broken again, and I just needed a friend to hold me and let me cry. Kathleen gave me the freedom to do that, too.

About a year before Kathleen retired, she told me about her plans to leave. I didn't let myself think about it then, not for a very long time. But all of a sudden, there it was – her retirement party. I said something at the gathering – I don't remember what – but it wasn't enough. Nothing I could have said would have been enough.

How could I adequately say "Thank you" for a lifetime of friendship, a lifetime of being there when I called out for help, a lifetime of listening, of understanding – and most of all, of making me feel I had worth?

Today Kathleen and I remain close. We have lunch together when our schedules allow, and we talk on the phone often. Kathleen stands ready to share my joys and sorrows in the deepest sense. She is a special friend who never ceases to enhance the quality of my life beyond measure.

A Friend Loves at All Times

The Bible says, "A friend loves at all times" (Proverbs 17:17). This being true, I am of all persons most blessed with friends.

"Robin, Maxine's chair died, and I can't lift her into her other chair," my mother explained on the phone. Robin, who lives three blocks away, was here in about two shakes, all the while teasing me about killing the chair just to bring him out in the middle of the night. Then there were the times he, Peggy, and Nichole took me to plays and restaurants and came to see me in the hospital three hours away. Robin mows the grass for us, washes our vehicles, cooks dinner for us, and finds a thousand other ways to show his family's friendship to us.

We call my morning helper "tall Wanda" (to differentiate her from my sister, "short Wanda"). Both Wandas get me out of bed and help me take a shower; then tall Wanda helps me get dressed for the day. I have lots of clothes, and she knows where every piece is. She does my hair exactly the way I like it. Best of all, we chat the whole time – the way friends do. Every morning she's there to share my joys ("I'm going to have lunch with Kathleen today" and my frustrations ("It aggravates me that these slacks I liked so much won't fit over the stupid pump"). And in the midst of all the morning hustle and bustle, she still takes time to give Sonny treats.

Just after my second pump surgery, I got cabin fever one morning and went to Wal-Mart, whereupon I suddenly realized that I needed to change clothes. Still extremely weak, I needed someone stronger than my mother to help me. Well, there in the middle of Wal-Mart stood Wanda! "I know you have to go back to work, but could you possibly come and help me change clothes?" I pleaded. I didn't have to plead. Wanda said, "Sure, I'll follow you home and we'll change." She makes everything so easy.

Marsha was Sonny's first girlfriend. She was a band student at Ole Miss when I got Sonny as a puppy. Every day Sonny and I passed through the band hall on the way to my office, and whenever Marsha was there, she gave Sonny a treat and accepted doggie kisses in return. Marsha married Keith, and the three of us became close friends. Marsha saw me through two surgeries, even helping Wanda wash my hair in bed using a baby swimming pool as a sink. When I was too sick to leave my sofa, Marsha came and sat with me and watched movies. With the birth of baby Lora Brooke, Marsha let me become "Aunt Mackie" to her as I joined in the fun of her first birthday party, trick-or-treating, and singing Christmas toys.

———

One afternoon there was a knock at my door and Ginny wheeled in. Remember, Ginny and I had been roommates at the long brick building when we were children. As adults, our lives forked in different directions, and we went for many years without seeing each other. Although we were in our 40s when we finally reconnected, it was almost as though no time had passed.

Ginny and I quickly renewed our friendship and discovered how much we had in common. We had both entered the world of computers – Ginny as a website developer and I as a software programmer and research analyst. We began working on various projects together; but best of all, we began encouraging each other to expand our horizons. I persuaded Ginny to acquire the equipment and software she needed to move her web design to new heights. In turn, Ginny used her tools and talents to design websites for me.

Our lives had come full circle. The young girl who had taken my braces off and rubbed baby oil on my blistered heel when no house mother would pay heed to my cries is now using her skills to help me tell my story to the world.

———

I've remained close to another friend from my days at the long brick building. Donnie and his wife Amy graciously let me borrow ideas from their specially built home when I was preparing to build mine. Then, in late 2007, Amy surprised me by nominating me for the Alumna of the Year for Mississippi State University's College of Education. Because of her and Donnie, I had the pleasure of being "Queen for a Day."

———

Awon and Anim, two wonderful young ladies from India, came to live with me during the spring semester of 2006. They took classes at Ole Miss and commuted there with me. At home they were impeccable housekeepers and eager helpers for me. A leaf couldn't touch the floor without being immediately swept away! And my calls for help were answered with the speed of lightning.

Today Awon and Anim are pursuing their education in Alabama. Awon attends a seminary, and Anim takes classes in cosmetology. We keep in touch, though, and they remain a special part of my group of friends.

In January 2008, the Hawaii International Conference on Education accepted a paper I had written for presentation at the conference. I was going to Hawaii!

Needing someone to travel with me, I advertised in our university's newspaper for a traveling companion. Laci answered the ad. She had been a student in my online class, but I had not met her face to face. After I did meet Laci, I knew that she wasn't just going for the "glamour" of a trip to Hawaii. She sincerely wanted to help me – lift me, bathe and dress me, feed me, and do all the other not-so-glamorous tasks involved in taking care of me.

We shared the Hawaii trip, all the way from the 9-hour flight with no accessible restroom to the late night walks around Honolulu. Best of all, though, we shared our lives and formed a lasting friendship that now includes Laci's husband Tyler. When we returned from Hawaii, Laci continued to be available when I needed a helping hand. Whenever I got a new assistant, Laci conveniently appeared to be sure things were going smoothly.

Weekly injections have been a part of my life almost since the time when rheumatoid arthritis invaded. Shelley, a nurse friend, has made the injection routine so much easier for me. She stops by every Monday evening after work to give me my shots and will never even consider letting me pay her. One evening Shelley told me about a mattress pad that allowed her son Austin, who also has cerebral palsy, to sleep more comfortably. Shelley's husband Mike immediately went and got one for me and put it on my bed. Shelley and Mike always say, "Don't hesitate to call us if you need anything."

When I began attending First Presbyterian Church, I gained a whole new set of friends. One of these friends, Larry, helps me get from Sunday School to church and then back to my van every Sunday. As director of buildings and grounds for the church, Larry was as excited as I was about the accessibility renovations to the church. We both smile when I wheel up the ramp to the folding doors and they automatically open for me.

Larry and his wife Rhea show their friendship to me in so many ways. Larry plants dozens of flowers in my flower bed in the spring time. He even made me an elegant bird feeder with a bright copper roof to hang outside my kitchen window. Rhea, a hairdresser, brings her shears to my house; and as much as I appreciate the haircuts, I appreciate even more the time we share together.

———

I know that a pastor is supposed to be everyone's friend, but I feel a special closeness with Rusty. My beloved Uncle Moss had been my pastor most of my life, so Rusty had a tough act to follow. But even before I joined First Presbyterian, Rusty saw me through one of the most difficult times in my life – the infamous breaking of the pump. Since then, Rusty has invited me to share my life story with many groups in the church, and he has always made me feel that my story was worth the telling. Not only that, he empathizes deeply with my plight while reassuring me that I'll be seated on the front pew in heaven! If that be the case, I look forward to sharing that pew with him and all my other friends and family.

Stuff Happens

I can get myself into some predicaments unlike anyone else.

It was Christmas Eve, and I almost burned the church down – not the little country church – the big church downtown. How did I manage that? Oh, it was pretty easy. I was attending the beautiful candlelight service – you know, the one where everybody holds an unlit candle and all the candles get lit while the congregation sings "Silent Night."

I was sitting in the back of the church, behind the last pew. Wanting to be polite, I took an unlit candle when it was offered. Nothing wrong with that, right? Wrong. My candle somehow got lit. I know now what "holy smoke" means because that's what I was thinking. My hand shook as the flame flickered. I stared at the flame and at my shaking hand.

What was I going to do with this candle? In my mind's eye I could see it falling to the floor and catching the whole church on fire. I could already hear the fire truck's siren and see people running out of the church screaming.

I looked around for someone to rescue me, but no one was looking my way. They were just sitting there singing as though there was nothing wrong! Meanwhile, the more frightened I became, the harder my hand shook and the harder my heart pounded.

Travis was standing in the back ushering. Finally I caught his eye, looked at the candle, and mouthed "Help!" He dashed over and took the candle from me as I breathed a sigh of relief and whispered "Thank you."

As I was leaving the cafeteria in the mall one Saturday, I'm not sure where my mind was, but apparently it wasn't on cerebral palsy. A friendly woman approached me and asked, "What do you have?" Thinking that her question was "What did you have," I smilingly told her "Meat loaf." Giving me a quizzical look, she said, "Well, I have MS," to which I quickly replied, "Oh, I have CP, but the meat loaf really is good."

My friend insisted on fixing me up with a guy she knew. "He really wants to meet you," she said as she brushed my hair and touched up my make-up. "He's waiting for us at the mall. Just give it a chance. You two may really hit it off," she urged.

So to the mall we went. Sure enough, there he was. My friend introduced us, then strolled down the mall, leaving us to get acquainted. It didn't take long.

"What do you do?" he began.

"I work at the university in the Center for Educational Research and Evaluation, and I teach an online course in special education."

"I don't like college," he stated.

I pressed on. "Well, I do a lot of statistics and writing. I spend most of the day at the computer."

"I hate computers," he told me matter-of-factly.

This was going nowhere fast. I decided it was time to change places. "Your job must be really interesting. What do you do?"

"I work on heavy equipment."

"My chair's pretty heavy. It weighs 250 pounds and has two car batteries in it."

This was turning out to be the longest 45 minutes in the history of 45 minutes. "My goodness," I said, looking at my watch. "It's already 9:00, and I have papers to grade."

I found my friend and said good-bye to my date. Back at home, my friend urged, "Why don't you call him and tell him what a nice time you had?"

Gulp.

Everyone loves my Twinkie story. Well, it goes like this. One night around midnight I was at home alone. My stomach started growling. I decided I was too hungry to sleep. But what could I get my hands on to eat? Aha! There on the kitchen table sat a Twinkie just staring at me. And miracle of miracles, it was unwrapped! Mine for the taking! "I can do it!" I reassured myself. "I can get that Twinkie and eat it." So I made a dive for it. I felt my hand wrap around the soft, golden sponge cake. I had it! Then, before I could get it to my mouth, I felt it go "Squish" as my hand tightened uncontrollably around that poor little cake. Crumbs began to fall, and the white gooey filling oozed out into my hand. Not one morsel made it to my mouth. My poor Twinkie ended up as a rubble of sticky goo.

I found out the hard way that the AutoZone in our historic Washington, DC looks amazingly like the AutoZone in my rural hometown. During my very first trip to Washington with my friend Sherry, I spent way too much of my time sitting in AutoZone while they attempted to recharge my wheelchair batteries. Yep, they died – right there in our nation's capital. So instead of seeing museums, I saw tires and car parts I didn't recognize – and didn't particularly want to learn about. Did they fix my chair? Nope. I had to be pushed through the airport manually – in my 250-pound chair. Not a good way to make friends in airports.

And speaking of airports, somehow I can never seem to get on or off an airplane without confusion. These airline episodes have become some of my favorite stories to tell.

My first flight took me to Miami Beach for a doctor's appointment. It was my first experience with the little carry-on chair. The attendants strapped me in and rolled me to my assigned seat at the back of the plane. After lifting me into the seat, they said, "We'll inform the in-flight attendants that you're a 'carry-off.'" Later, as the flight ended and we came in for a landing, a smiling young woman in an airline uniform made her way down the aisle toward me.

"You're a carry-off?" she questioned.

"Yes, ma'am," I replied.

"Well," she said, "it would help us a whole lot if you could just walk to that door at the front of the plane."

Replying that I was unable to oblige, I couldn't help thinking, "Yeah, it would help me a whole lot, too!"

On another flight I happened to be traveling home alone. I was waiting in line with all the others who need to board first. A gentleman approached me and said, "I'll be happy to carry you onto the plane. My wife is in a wheelchair, too, so I know how to do this." Not being one to turn down offers of help, I graciously accepted. When my turn came, the guy picked me up in his arms. As my face came closer to his, I noticed that his breath smelled strongly of liquor. The man wasn't intoxicated; he was drunk. The thought ran through my mind, "I can't walk and neither can you!"

Mercifully, we made it onto the plane intact. Unfortunately, we didn't have assigned seats, so the guy insisted on sitting beside me. During the one-hour flight, he ordered two more drinks. "Oh, great!" I thought. "Just what he needs!"

"Will someone be at the airport to meet you?" he asked.

"Oh, yes, my sister will be there," I replied, thinking, "Wanda, if you're ever late in your life, please don't let it be now."

Well, the guy was even more drunk when we landed, but he insisted on carrying me off the plane. To my great relief, Wanda was there waiting. She quickly realized what was going on, and we hurriedly escaped to the baggage claim area. But there he was, too. "Oh, good," he said, "I was afraid I wasn't going to get my kiss."

As we finally walked away, I moaned, "I finally get kissed and it has to be by a drunk."

The words no one who uses a wheelchair wants to hear: "Are you sure you had a wheelchair with you when you came on the plane? We can't seem to find it."

The other words no one who is being carried down the steps of a plane wants to hear: "This isn't working. What should we do?" Worse yet is hearing the response: "Pick it up and run with it!" – knowing you're it!

God Is Always Watching and Listening

One of the unique benefits of being in a helpless state is that the master Helper always stands ready to help. He has come to my aid countless times, often even before I had time to ask.

One afternoon on my commute home from Delta State, the van sputtered and died about 10 miles from my house. There was no one riding that day except Mark and me. Mark steered the van over onto the shoulder of the road. We were trying to decide whether Mark should leave me and go for help when a car pulled up behind us and a man got out. It was my Uncle Macey. "Looks like y'all need a ride," he grinned. At that, he picked me up and set me on the front seat of his car. Then he folded my wheelchair and put it in the trunk. As we were riding home, I teased Uncle Macey, "I guess God sent you along because He figured I wouldn't fare very well as a hitchhiker."

Finding someone to drive the 180-mile commute to Ole Miss with me has been a constant challenge. However, God has always provided. One summer, though, a sudden and unexpected problem arose, and I needed a driver the next day – and for the rest of the summer. Not knowing exactly what to do, I went for a walk with Sonny. As I reached the edge of the driveway, my friend and neighbor Lane drove by. He stopped and asked how I was doing. "Well, I've been better," I began. Then I proceeded to tell him my troubles. I was telling the right person! He quickly said, "I can help." As a school band director, he had some available days during the summer, so we made some quick arrangements for Lane and my cousin Phil to rotate days driving me to work. I rode home with a song of thanksgiving in my heart for this miraculous answer to my need. A most enjoyable added benefit of this arrangement was developing a closer friendship with Lane. By the way, for anyone who doubts the caregiving abilities of men, both Lane and Phil are terrific at taking care of me, including feeding me.

My cousin Emmy says that every woman would appreciate my bathroom story. (If you're a man, you can still read it.) I had placed an ad in the Ole Miss newspaper for a personal assistant (actually meaning someone to help me in the restroom). Well, one day I was especially in need of that "someone," but I wasn't sure where she would come from. All of a sudden, in walked one of my former students. It wasn't just any student, though. It was Stacy. You'd have to know Stacy. Nothing ruffled her. She said, "Hey, lady. How ya doing? Was that your ad in the paper? What kind of help do you need?" Sheepishly, I told her. She put her hands on her hips and said, "Well, do you need to go now?" I nodded "yes," to which she replied, "Well, let's go then." God didn't just send someone; he sent the right someone. When I told Emmy this story, she said, "Now every time I go to the restroom, I'll say a prayer that if you're needing to go, God will send someone to help you."

I suppose God knows by now that He needs to be on special standby during candlelight Christmas Eve services. After the fiasco when I almost dropped a burning candle, I wisely chose not to hold a candle again. But one Christmas Eve when all the candles were lit and we were singing, I felt kind of lonely without a candle. I silently prayed that someone would come up and hold a candle for me. A moment later, I felt a hand on my shoulder, and I saw a lighted candle beside me. John, who was ushering that night, had stepped up beside me and was holding a candle for me. When I told Pastor Rusty about it, he said, "Thanks for sharing that story with me....ole John certainly caught the meaning of Christmas incarnation...reaching out in a real and tangible way and sharing God's love....a small but significant way....and much appreciated."

I believe that every day a new story could be added to this chapter. Well, here's one more. I was running out of time to find an outfit for a very special occasion – the photograph for the cover of this book! Phil drove me to a department store an hour away and turned me loose. He would have been glad to help, but after all, how much help can a guy be when it comes to ladies clothes?

I decided to make a quick swing through the store just to get an idea of what I had to choose from. As I was making my round, a kind sales lady named Minor walked up and asked if she could help me. My eyes brightened as I said, "You certainly can – that is, if you have time."

Then I heard something I never expected to hear. Minor said, "Actually, I was a little bored. I was just doing some straightening up until someone came along who needed my help."

Immediately we began chatting about the type of outfit I wanted. It was then that I realized something even more remarkable than Minor's availability. She understood every word I said!

Minor and I traversed the store together for an hour. During that time we selected two sweater sets and a pair of jeans. We were both delighted with our selections, but even more delighted with the new friendships we had formed. Although shopping is one of my favorite things to do, it often reminds me of how dependent I am on family members and friends to help me. That day, though, I felt so proud of being able to carry on a normal, successful dialogue with a stranger whom God placed in my path to become my friend.

Strength in Weakness

I'd always thought my speech was a weakness – that is, until I learned how it helped a friend understand her mother's dying words.

You see, the cerebral palsy that strains my limbs also strains my voice. The air that tries to come up through my throat is squeezed so tightly that it sounds almost like I have a kerchief tied around my neck. My lips and my tongue find their way to the correct place with much effort, making my words sound distorted. Those accustomed to my speech have little trouble understanding me, but those who are with me less often must listen more carefully to understand. I always considered this a hindrance, a burden.

Then one night Emmy called to tell me that one of her best friends had lost her mother. "Maxine," she said, "it meant so much to my friend that she had learned to listen so carefully to your speech. As her mother grew weaker and weaker, it became harder to understand what she was saying. But because of you, my friend knew how to listen, and she was blessed with the invaluable gift of understanding what her mother was saying in her dying days."

As I reflected on the weak, halting speech of which I was so ashamed, I remembered the words spoken by the Lord to the apostle Paul – "My strength is made perfect in weakness." (II Corinthians 12:9)

My Daddy

His given name is Maxie Allen Harper, but to me he's Daddy. None of this "Father" or "Dad" stuff. He has always been and will forever be my "Daddy."

My first real memory of Daddy is when I was a three-year-old, being held all night in his lap because I was too sick to lie down flat in my bed. He took me on my first visit to the dentist and held me in his lap as the dentist used the tooth polisher to gently polish my nails. I remember, too, that wherever we went, I hung around Daddy's neck like a baby gorilla. He carried me until I was so tall that my feet touched the floor.

One of my favorite memories, though, was the time I was sitting outside in my wheelchair with Daddy as he worked on his fishing tackle. Most other 9-year-olds were riding their bikes around the neighborhood while I slowly maneuvered my chair across the patio with my feet. My frustration spilled over as I said, "I wish I could ride a bike." Daddy said nothing. But the episode remained on his mind.

One afternoon a few weeks later, when Daddy arrived home from work, he asked me to go outside with him for a minute. He wheeled me down the ramp; and there, sitting in the back yard, was a golf cart that Daddy had bought for his girls to ride in.

We painted the golf cart yellow and dotted it with bright yellow and orange stick-on hippie flowers. Wanda and I, with Spot in the middle, rode that golf cart all over the neighborhood, with Spot barking furiously at anyone who dared come close.

Later Daddy bought a mobile home on a lake for a weekend getaway. He had the mobile home customized with wide doorways for my wheelchair. Down the hill, on the edge of the lake, a long wooden pier stretched out into the water. We spent many an hour fishing from that pier. Daddy also bought a pontoon so I could sit in a chair and ride across the lake, trolling for crappie as we went. Many nights we baited trotlines and went back the next morning to see what we had caught. I can still see Daddy pulling large catfish off the hook.

The golf cart and the "cabin" live on in my memory as a symbol – a symbol that someone believed I deserved the same freedoms and pleasures as all other persons. My Daddy wanted me to have a bicycle and a camping experience like other kids. He had to be extraordinarily creative and dedicated to give me those things; but in doing so, he was giving me something even more important. He was giving me his genuine love and respect.

Throughout my life, Daddy has always been so proud of my accomplishments. When I was named valedictorian, I called him at work and said, "Daddy, I'm the valedictorian!" His reply of "Girl!" said it all. When I was working on my doctorate degree, he and Mama spent many an hour driving me 45 miles to class and making copies of articles in the library. I could feel their joy as I received a standing ovation at graduation. Whenever an article was printed about me in the newspaper, Daddy would come home with an armload of papers.

Daddy's commitment to my education was always special to me. When I was still a baby, Daddy tried to buy life insurance for both Wanda and me. Wanda was accepted; I wasn't. No matter – I was going to live, and I was going to college. To prove it, Daddy started saving for me, as well as Wanda, to go to college.

Daddy wanted his girls' lives to be easier than his had been. He grew up during the Great Depression, when he and his brothers had to help farm the land in order to have food to eat. Daddy laughingly recalls the time when he and his brother were fussing. Their mother said, "Okay, boys, kiss and make up," to which Daddy replied, "I'd rather kiss Ole Blue (the family dog)."

Daddy attended a small country school and graduated as valedictorian of his class. Then, in need of work, he joined the Civilian Conservation Corps, planting pine trees and digging trenches to prevent soil erosion. He sent home most of the money he earned. Never having been away from his family, Daddy felt the sharp pains of homesickness. Still, he fulfilled his three months of service and even reenlisted for another six-month tour. Since money was extremely scarce, Daddy once noticed that a postage stamp on a letter he had received from home had not been postmarked, so he reused it to send a letter back home.

After his nine months in the CCC, Daddy attended Draughn's Business College and then worked as a bookkeeper for the McCain Estate in Carroll County. Later Daddy attended Aurora College in Illinois for a semester before returning home to enlist in the armed services.

During World War II, Daddy joined what was called the Army Air Forces. After a few months of training, he was assigned to the B29 Bomber Squadron and flew to Tinian Island. He laughs about the time when he was in his tent and one of his buddies came to him and announced, "The lieutenant wants to see you." Daddy jokingly said, "Well, tell him to be 'At Ease.'" His buddy yelled, "Shut up, you fool! He's standing right here."

As it turned out, the lieutenant wanted Daddy to help him set up and operate a PX. In the process, the lieutenant and my Daddy became fast friends, and at night they often walked to a nearby marine base and watched movies.

Another good friend during Daddy's military days was a Major Berry, the squadron doctor. The Major, though, was soon transferred from Tinian to Iwo Jima. A few weeks after his transfer, a plane was scheduled to leave Tinian carrying some equipment to Iwo Jima. Without Daddy knowing it, Major Berry had arranged for Daddy to be on that flight. When the plane landed on Iwo Jima, Daddy found the Major and visited with him before flying back to Tinian the next day. Friendships like these were precious to Daddy.

While Daddy was serving overseas, his own father became terminally ill with cancer, and Daddy received emergency leave so he could return home and help care for him. After his father died, Daddy completed his tour of duty and finally came home to Mississippi for good.

When Daddy and Mama met and married, he was living in Greenwood with his brother Moss and his family. Uncle Moss performed the wedding ceremony for Mama and Daddy in 1951, and I would say he tied a very good knot!

Daddy was at that time office manager for the Butane Gas Company of Greenwood. He was soon promoted to company manager, a job he held for more than 30 years. Daddy was good at his job, and he cared about his employees. One cold Christmas morning Daddy was busy putting together a doll house when a customer called and needed a tank of gas brought to his house. Rather than call a delivery man out on Christmas, Daddy delivered the gas himself. (I still wonder if that wasn't easier than putting together the doll house.)

Daddy's company had an irrigation department, and Daddy learned to design impressively complex center pivot irrigation systems. During dry summer months it was hard to keep up with the demand, and even today I can see Daddy standing on our front porch praying for rain to take some of the pressure off as one farmer after another pleaded to be next in line to have an irrigation system installed.

Daddy retired in 1983 with the title Vice President and General Manager. It was then that he went to work doing what he loves to do best – taking care of his girls. I remember his saying, "I didn't retire; I just changed careers."

Daddy turned 90 years old on February 18, 2008. He still takes care of me. He sees that the oil in my van is changed on time and that we never run out of Cokes in the fridge. He cooks my favorite foods – catfish and hush puppies, fried green tomatoes, chicken and dressing, and creamed corn. He likes to tease me about my bargain shopping. One day I brought home a shirt that cost all of $3. When I told Daddy about it, he said, "Watch out. The police will be after you for stealing."

Especially dear to me, though, is Daddy's love for Sonny and the special care he takes of him. Daddy prepares a special diet for "his boy" and freezes the food in cartons. Every morning Sonny listens for the last ding of the microwave, signaling that breakfast is ready. Sonny jumps off my bed and runs to the kitchen, where I hear Daddy say, "Well, there's my little bitty boy." Then, when Sonny is ready to play Frisbee, Daddy says, "Let me get my jacket and we'll play." Daddy tosses the Frisbee into the air; Sonny runs after it, jumps high, catches it, and lopes back with the Frisbee in his mouth. Daddy claps his hands and gives the Frisbee another toss.

My Sister

It was another Sunday during my stay at the long brick building. I'd heard that a ruling had come down saying that siblings couldn't come to visit. When my parents arrived to take me out for the afternoon, I immediately asked, "Where's Wanda?" Daddy put a finger to his lips, saying "Shhh!" But I was persistent. "Where's Wanda?" I wanted to know. Finally we got to the car and Daddy explained, "We dropped Wanda and Pappy off at the Tote-Sum store around the corner, and we're going to pick them up right now. You'll see Wanda in just a minute." I smiled at their scheme.

For four very long years, I saw Wanda only on Sundays and during my quarterly vacations at home. I missed her. When Mama and Daddy finally consented to let me stay at home, I went to the bedroom that Wanda and I would now share, and I said simply, "I don't have to go back." She knew the rest of the sentence – "ever again." We were both happy.

But how does an 8-year-old get to know a 7-year-old sister who doesn't really remember when they lived together? Wanda and I weren't strangers, but we weren't close friends either. We slowly, gradually made our way into each other's life. Both of us liked Barbie dolls, so Wanda collected Barbie and Midge, and I collected Ken and Allen, with all their accessories. We enjoyed the music groups of the day, like the Beatles and the Monkees. What we enjoyed most, though, was riding around the neighborhood in the golf cart that Daddy bought for us.

Unfortunately, for the first three years after I came home, Wanda and I weren't able to go to the same school. Barred from sharing school experiences, we had less to talk about than other siblings so close in age. I didn't know who Mrs. Jackson was, and I couldn't fully appreciate the antics of boys I hadn't met. We did share a few friends who came to our house and played Monopoly with us.

When we finally began going to the same school, Wanda and I were in the same grade from 6th grade on. Wanda was, of course, part of my support team. She was among those who rolled my wheelchair and typewriter from class to class, and she shared her notes from the classes we had alike. Best of all, we were finally able to sit around the kitchen table after school and share common happenings of the day. "What are you going to do your book report on?"; "I need a butterfly for my insect collection; so if you find another one, catch it for me"; "There's a ginkgo tree in the courthouse yard. Let's get leaves there for our leaf collection." Okay, if this is beginning to sound too much like Leave It To

Beaver, I suppose it was. But it was a family life with my sister that I wasn't sure we would ever share.

After graduation, though, Wanda and I went to different colleges, and once again we led very different lives. Wanda attended Mississippi College, a Baptist school 100 miles away. She lived in the dorm, joined a sorority, and developed close friendships. I could tell she was enjoying spreading her wings. She found her niche in art and graphic design, and in the summers she apprenticed in our hometown under one of the gurus in the field.

Wanda and I graduated from college one week apart – in May of 1978. After college Wanda continued to spread her wings, getting a job with an advertising firm in Jackson, not too far from the college where she had graduated. She loved having her own apartment. I think it was then that she began developing her culinary talent. As with everything else, "ordinary" cooking didn't appeal to Wanda. She liked to experiment with recipes and make her own special dishes. She also developed a love for plants and herbs, evidenced by the tiny garden on her patio.

In 1980, Wanda's mentor from our hometown invited her to come and work for him, so she came back to live and work in Greenwood. With her lived a beautiful, deep red golden retriever, Gip (named after Pappy, whom everyone else called Gip). Gip knew his way around town quite well. Sometimes he would decide to go downtown to Wanda's office and sit in her parking space and wait for her.

Shortly after Wanda moved back, she and Travis started dating. In March of 1984, they came to the house and said to Mama and Daddy, "We've decided to give you an anniversary present and get married on your anniversary."

After Wanda married, I began to think, "Okay, it's time for me to be an aunt." In December 1986, Wanda and Travis broke the news – Wanda was pregnant! I squealed with delight and gave her a hug. Since Wanda and I had never really talked about my condition, in the back of my mind I wondered if even the remote possibility of having a child with a disability would trouble her. I was so proud of her when she told me that she saw no need to have the tests to determine whether the baby had any abnormalities. "We're just gonna take what we get," she said.

What they got was a perfectly beautiful baby girl with reddish blond hair and blue eyes. They named her Avent – a family name on Travis's side. Our love for Avent gave Wanda and me a more intimate bond than we had ever had before. Our cousin Linda kept Avent during the day while Wanda worked, and often in the evenings I rode with Wanda and Travis out to Linda's house in the country to get Avent. That was a special time for me as they allowed me to be part of their family. They continued to include me in their lives, from Christmas Eve dinners for their church friends to Avent's school plays and dance recitals. At one Christmas Eve dinner, Wanda had not had much preparation time, so Avent's room wasn't exactly ready for inspection. When one of the guests asked Avent to let her see her room, Avent said matter-of-factly, "I can't. My Mama told me not to open that door."

Wanda's graphic design talent merged with my writing when we published *Daffodils in the Snow*. Wanda designed the cover and did the layout for the book. I loved working with her on the mutual project, and this earth has not known two parents more proud than ours. During the process of having the book printed, the printer e-mailed me one day and asked if I saw Wanda very often. He wanted to know if we would have a chance to get together on a decision about the weight of paper we wanted to use. I laughed because what he didn't know was that at that time I was seeing Wanda three times a day (my van was in the shop, and she was driving me to and from work in her car).

Especially distinctive about Wanda is her love for animals. When we were young, she had ducks, goldfish, and a rabbit. She began with one Easter duck and then inherited three more from children whose parents decided they didn't need their ducks. After a few months, we had to find a nice farm for four very large ducks! Today Wanda has three large dogs – one that was supposed to be a golden retriever and somehow turned out to be a miniature deer, and two others of unknown pedigree that she took in off the streets. She adores them all.

Wanda thrives on uniqueness. She has earned the title "Little Debbie Queen" around her office because of her love for Little Debbie snacks. That's all she ever eats for breakfast. During one Christmas when we had company for dinner, Wanda concocted a trifle made from Little Debbie orange-cranberry muffins. Little Debbie would be proud!

More than making Little Debbie proud, Wanda has made me proud of her in ways that she may have considered small, but they were significant to me. When I was in the hospital for my pump implant, the nurses wanted to give my medicine on their schedule, not necessarily when I needed it. Wanda politely offered to give me my medicine herself, but the nurses refused, saying that they had a one-hour leeway (early or late) in giving medicine. Normally very compliant, Wanda took a stand on my behalf, realizing that if I didn't get my medicine on time, my spasticity would get out of hand. She said firmly, "Well, Maxine doesn't have a one-hour leeway, so you can either give her medicine on time or I'll give it to her." The next morning, the head nurse walked into my room with her hands up in surrender and apology. From then on, I got my medicine exactly on time.

Now, at First Presbyterian Church, where Wanda and I are both members, Wanda sometimes serves Communion. On Sunday, November 23, 2008, she happened to be assigned to my pew for the first time. There was something indescribably special about hearing her say, "This is Christ's body broken for you" and having her place the bread in my mouth and then hearing her say, "This is Christ's blood shed for you" and having her put the cup to my lips. We are not only blood sisters; we are sisters in Christ.

Avent

It was early December 1986, and brother-in-law Travis had just returned from a Chicago business trip. He brought with him three identically wrapped Christmas gifts, one for Mama, one for Daddy, and one for me. Travis insisted that we open our gifts "now." Daddy opened his first. It was a green terry cloth square with the words "Ho! Ho! Ho!" written in red across the front. Turning it over in his hands, Daddy tried to guess what it was. "A shoe shine rag?" he queried. Nope. When Mama and I opened our gifts to find the same green terry cloth Christmas item, Mama gave a puzzled look. Then I screamed! Those were bibs! Wanda was pregnant!

My joy knew no bounds. I was going to be an aunt! I remember thinking, though, that I had an impossible act to follow. Who could measure up to Aunt Elma? Still, I put my whole heart into this new role. In late February, I found myself smiling at Wanda's slightly pooching middle. I cherished her baby showers, especially the one at our little church, where Daddy and Travis sat up front, waiting to carry the loot away.

Wanda would be giving birth in Jackson, two hours away. What elaborate plans we made! When the time came, we would caravan – just in case Travis had a flat tire or other unforeseen car trouble. But that wasn't necessary. At Wanda's last doctor's appointment, she was ordered to remain in Jackson. The baby could come any time. Sure enough, Wanda went into labor that evening, and Avent was delivered by C-section the next morning, Friday, August 7, 1987.

Secretly I had hoped for a girl, though I knew I couldn't let it be known. A little boy would be fine, but I had drooled over those frilly little girl clothes. I was one happy aunt when I first held my porcelain doll niece. A few hours after Avent was born, we left the hospital to let Wanda get some rest. But we returned on Saturday and again on Sunday, each time bearing sweet little "bubble suits" of pink and white. Wanda kept Avent with her all the time – usually cuddled up in bed with her – which brought about lots of teasing from the nurses.

We expected Wanda to come home on Wednesday with her new bundle, so we were pleasantly surprised when she and Travis walked in the back door on Tuesday night and Travis set the infant seat on the kitchen table. I peeked over and saw blankets aplenty folded in the carrier, but it was Avent I wanted to see. Finally I found her, a little wad scrunched down in the bottom of the seat, sound asleep.

Our cousin Linda was the chosen one to care for Avent while Wanda worked, and no one could have been more perfect. Linda was totally devoted to Avent. They rocked by the hour in the big rocking chair by the window, and many nights when I made the 17-mile drive with Wanda and Travis to pick Avent up from Linda's house I'd smile to see a baby bottle sitting in the window. The trip home was always special because I could gaze at Avent to my heart's content. I made a valiant effort to sing to her "I love you a bushel and a peck."

Avent was a fun baby, loving to play but not liking to sleep. Neither did she like high chairs or strollers. And I think her first word was "down." I'll always remember the first time she said my name. Daddy was driving the van, and Mama was holding Avent in her lap on the front seat. My wheelchair was parked in the middle, behind the two front seats. All of a sudden, Avent looked back at me and said, "Mackie!" My smile was so wide I thought it would crack my face.

I loved every age Avent ever was. I loved the first time we tried keeping her all night. Wanda was sure Avent would fall asleep before she returned, and Avent was just as sure she would stay awake. Wanda had told us to leave a light on in one room of the house as a signal for her to stop and retrieve her baby if necessary. As midnight approached, Avent was not even close to falling asleep. Daddy took no chances. Wanda returned to find every light in the house burning brightly. She teased Daddy about his lack of subtlety, to which Daddy replied, "I was getting ready to build a fire in the front yard."

Avent showed an early fondness for driving. When she was about 6 months old, we were coming back from the mall, which was about an hour away. Suddenly she began to cry inconsolably. Wanda pulled off the highway, took Avent out of her car seat and stood her up in her lap to try to figure out what she wanted. Avent grabbed the steering wheel, then looked back at Wanda and grinned. Ah, yes, she wanted to drive!

Avent was fun at age 1, carrying around her stuffed animal "Puff" as she took her first faltering steps, then as she learned to walk, run, and climb. She was fun at age 2, when Santa brought her a Barbie swimming pool and she insisted on going swimming in the living room on Christmas day. I laughed when Avent, at age 3, ate turnip greens with her fingers.

I felt immense satisfaction when Avent, at age 4, wanted to play the three wishes game with my mother, whom Avent calls Mimi. Avent wished for toys (I can't imagine a toy she didn't have). Mimi's wish was harder to fill. She wished that Mackie could walk. After pondering the idea, Avent said thoughtfully, "That would be nice, but I like her just the way she is."

Still, Avent wanted me to be able to do everything she could do. At an early age, she didn't know why walking was all that hard for me. She tried to explain, "It's easy … you just put one foots right here and one foots right there and" (holding out her hands) "that's all there is to it!" She also thought it would be easy to make my hands work right. One day she brought out two sheets of paper and told me to put my hands on them. Her plan was simple. "I'm going to cut out some good hands for you." Wonder why I hadn't thought of that!

Avent grew up before my eyes. I attended her very long dance recitals and her funny school plays. I helped her find missing pieces to her soccer uniform (she called it her "costume"). I helped her write lyrics to a Halloween poem for school. She helped me open the gifts at my housewarming party. When she unwrapped the can opener, she said with delight, "We needed one of these."

I loved the summer when Avent helped me in my office downtown. She was about 11 and could answer the phone, use the fax machine, and do some filing. Mostly I enjoyed her company. A restaurant down the street had delicious chocolate cake, and often Avent would walk over and get a piece for us. We'd eat it in the conference room while we talked over the business of the day.

Now in college, Avent has truly flourished. I puffed with pride as I saw her walk across the football field as Sophomore Homecoming Maid. And I delighted in her appointment as Student Activities Director and then as Chief of Staff to the Student Body President. She has been a leader in a variety of Christian activities, including Campus Crusade for Christ and Greek Summit. While she was attending a retreat several years ago, I wrote her a letter whose words remain fitting today.

July 27, 2004

Dear Avent,

I'm sitting here wondering how I can put into words 17 years of feeling the love I have for you, the joy you bring me, and the pride I have in you. I fell in love with you the very first time I laid eyes on you, and for all the years of your life you've brought me a very special joy. Getting to be with you as you've grown up has been the best part of my life. I loved just sitting and watching you when you were a baby; I loved playing with you when you were a little girl; and as you've become a young woman, I've loved being with you and sharing the things that make you happy, because they make me happy, too.

I am so very proud to be your aunt - your Mackie. I do feel such pride in you and in who you are. You're kind and gentle, loving and compassionate, strong and sure of yourself, and committed to what you believe. You are your own person, and what a wonderful person you are!

Often I talk about you as though I were talking about my own daughter. And the way my face lights up, people always guess that we do have a special relationship. So I wish for you just what I would wish for a daughter- a life filled with love, happiness, and God's richest blessings.

Love,
Mackie

Mama

"Mama!" I must have called her name thousands of times over the course of my life – and she has always answered.

When I was very little, I would call during the night, "Mama, cover me up." Or I would say from my standing box, "Mama, take me out. My legs are tired." During the mosquito-ridden summers, I would often plead, "Mama, scratch my mosquito bites."

When I was away at the long brick building, every Sunday I would try to position myself so I could see down the long corridor into the lobby and get the first glimpse of Mama when she came in. She looked pretty in her pleated skirts, with her light brown hair pulled back in a roll. Mama was determined to see me every Sunday, no matter what. One Sunday Daddy had the flu and the ground was covered with snow, but even that didn't deter Mama; she caught a ride with another family.

It's strange the little things you remember. One Sunday I was sick and couldn't go out of the building, so we had to visit in the therapy room. I remember Mama holding me and putting her cheek against mine to see if I had fever.

During my four year stay at the long brick building, Mama went back to work as a secretary, which had been her career before she had children. As Lela "Bernice" Gibson, she had attended Draughn's Business College before going to work at Camp McCain, a World War II army base. Mama remembers going to dances for the soldiers and then having to wave good-bye to them as they left on buses going to the war zone. Mama loved working at the camp and was obviously very good at her job because she was the last female employee to leave when the camp closed. She then moved to Greenwood, where she met and married Daddy and continued working as a secretary until I was born.

When I came home from the long brick building, Mama quit work to care for me. That was probably a greater sacrifice than she ever admitted, because she absolutely loved being a secretary. However, she put all her energy into motherhood – into seeing that Wanda and I had everything we needed – and wanted.

We were a Coke drinking family; and in those days Coke bottles were recycled. I can still see Mama loading the station wagon with cases of Coke bottles to return to the store. Mama liked to bake, and she usually had homemade goodies waiting for us when we got home from school. My favorite was her gingerbread with lemon sauce. Mama made snack time a memorably pleasant part of the day, when we could unwind from our school activities, satisfy our afternoon hunger, and share stories from school. Then, on Saturday mornings, Mama would get fresh doughnuts for breakfast, and we'd eat outside on the patio.

The ordinary motherhood role of chauffeur was intensified for Mama. Before we got a van, Mama took me to school in the car. That meant lifting me onto the seat of the car, folding my chair and putting it behind the front seat, then taking the chair out and setting me in it when we got to school. The whole process had to be repeated when she took me home. Getting a van made the process a little easier, but not much. Pappy built a wooden ramp with hinges in the middle to let it fold. Mama had to unfold and let down the heavy ramp, roll me into the van, then lift and fold the ramp. Once again, this was a double process, since she then had to get me out of the van. Every school day Mama went through this routine three times – morning, noon, and afternoon. Finally, when I was in high school, she was able to cut back to morning and early afternoon. Still, it was a rigorous routine, and I can count on one hand the number of days she missed due to illness. Mama just didn't get sick!

Every day after school, Mama assumed her role as my scribe. Even though I typed some of my homework myself, I could not possibly have typed it all. So Mama and I sat at the card table for hours, and Mama wrote as I dictated to her. She wrote exactly what I said, almost oblivious to what she was writing. Her job was just to get the stuff on paper for me, not to learn it or even understand it. Looking back, I appreciate so much the fact that Mama expected me to use my own mind; she just let me borrow her hands. Yet, every year on Awards Day, she must have felt an extra surge of pride, knowing that she played a special part in the awards I received.

One particularly vivid memory I have is of Mama standing on a ladder in the back yard one night with a net swinging in her hand as she tried to catch a moth for my insect collection. Now, you would have to know Mama to really understand what an act of love that was. Mama cared not one whit for bugs, and she cared even less for climbing ladders. But she did it for me. And, by the way, I (or I should say "we") received the Biology award that year.

During my childhood, Mama had only a few activities outside the home that she enjoyed. She played bridge with a group of ladies once a month, and she loved going to the annual conventions on the Mississippi Gulf Coast with Daddy.

After I graduated from high school, Mama drove me to the community college 25 miles away every day for two semesters. But when I began commuting to Delta State, 45 miles away, we enlisted carpoolers to drive. Even then, Mama was always waiting when I got home – waiting to feed me a late lunch or help me with whatever I needed.

After college, my first job was to serve on a committee that met every Friday in Yazoo City, about 50 miles away. Mama drove me there and waited all day while I worked. She passed the time by doing needlepoint and shopping.

Mama continued to be my hands and legs during my school teaching years. She drove me to work and picked me up in the afternoons. By this time, I had a power chair, and we had a van with an automatic lift. Taking me places had finally gotten easier.

When I entered the doctoral program at Delta State, Mama and Daddy spent hours driving me to night classes and feeding dimes into the library copier. As I neared the completion of my degree, I submitted rough drafts of my dissertation from the computer in dot matrix print. But the final copy had to be typed – and typed precisely to APA specifications, with exact margins on all four sides, no "orphan" line at the bottom of a page, and on and on. Typically, only "professionals" who were accustomed to the regulations dared tackle the daunting task. However, the person who usually typed dissertations wasn't available, so it was Mama to the rescue – again. "I'll type it," she offered. "I know I can do it." I knew she could, too. What we hadn't anticipated, though, was that in the midst of the process, Pappy became seriously ill and passed away. Despite her shock and grief, Mama immediately plunged back into her typing task. She typed my dissertation to perfection, tedious data tables and all.

At graduation, when I received my doctorate, I loved seeing the joy on the faces of Mama and Daddy as I passed by them after my hooding and my standing ovation. I wrote in my dissertation acknowledgments that three degrees should be awarded – one for me and one for each of my parents.

Later, when I worked in software development, Mama drove me all over the state as I installed our software in schools from one corner of the state to the other. She even went with me to Florida and Texas in my software distribution forays.

Mama has played a huge part in all my ventures. When I built my house, Mama took me to search for just the right brick, just the right roof shingles, just the right floor coverings, and just the right paint and wallpaper. To Mama's credit, she has always respected – and, in fact, made possible – my independent thinking.

During the publication of *Daffodils in the Snow*, Mama worked diligently to help me get ISBNs and barcodes and do all the other leg work involved in self-publishing. I loved seeing her sheer delight as she held book after book for me to sign.

Mama has been there through all the seasons of my life. She shared the joy of my first trip to DisneyWorld, my starting a new business, my getting a job at Ole Miss, my becoming Mom to Sonny. She shared the sorrow of my losing the use of my legs, the trials of my first pump surgery, the terror of the catheter to the pump breaking, and my struggle to recover and move forward.

Mama has done everything in her power to enhance the quality of my life. She has been relentless in seeing that I get whatever I need to make me more comfortable. When a new drug was released for rheumatoid arthritis, Mama called every pharmacy in town until she found one that would order the medicine for me. When a wheelchair was delivered to me with the wrong specifications, Mama rose to her full 5-foot height and insisted that the technician get his measuring tape. After measuring the chair, he had to admit, "You're right, ma'am. The chair is 3 ½ inches higher than it's supposed to be." After the guy left, a friend who was here said, "Your mother sure got in his face. I've never seen her eyes blaze like that!"

Yes, I'll always remember the big, important events that Mama and I have shared. But even more, I'll always remember the little ways she has had of saying, "I love you and I want you to be happy." She said it in the chocolate Coca-Cola sheet cake, in the tiny sapphire and diamond ring, in the cross-stitched Bible verse that hangs above my bed, and in the pink jacket she likes to see me wear. She said it by always being there and answering whenever I called "Mama!"

In My Dreams

The alarm clock buzzed softly. I reached over and turned it off before it woke Ross. There was time to let him sleep a few more minutes. Besides, I liked waking him myself.

Lying back on my pillow, I thanked God for the new day before me, for the family with whom I would share it. I looked over at Ross still sleeping peacefully. His thick dark hair was graying ever so slightly at the temples. His face had a gentle ruggedness that reflected a personality filled with resolve yet tender enough to bottle feed a newborn puppy that had lost its mother.

Ross and I had met in graduate school. I was immediately attracted to his "realness." He had no desire to put on a front; in fact, I don't think he could even if he wanted to. He wasn't like any man I'd ever known. I had dated a little in high school, but most of my dates were group dates, and there was certainly no boy I was serious about. In college I still found most of the guys to be superficial and very caught up in themselves. There wasn't one that really interested me.

Then in graduate school Ross and I had a class together called "Emotional Dynamics of Learning Disabilities." It was a 600 level doctoral course that we were both required to take – I for my doctorate in Special Education and he for his doctorate in Counseling. We both thought the class was pretty difficult, mainly because it was so technical, almost like a class in medical school. So we began studying together. Some nights we ended up just talking, though.

Ross and I had both moved to Chapel Hill from small towns pretty far away. My family was in Mississippi and his was in Tennessee. We had been in Chapel Hill only a few months; and we hadn't gotten to know many people yet, so we became close friends. We both enjoyed cooking, and many evenings we spent in the kitchen at his apartment or mine trying out new dishes. As we cooked, we laughed and talked. We shared our pasts and our hopes for the future.

We were married the summer after we received our degrees. It was a small wedding attended by only close family and friends. My only sister was my matron of honor, and Ross's dad was his best man. We went to Canada for our honeymoon. Neither of us had ever traveled outside the states, and we had both heard of Canada's beautiful, clean countryside. We rented a car and just drove through Canada sightseeing and talking.

Back in Chapel Hill, Ross and I bought a three-bedroom home on a quiet cul de sac near the university where we had both graduated and gotten teaching positions. We knew we wanted to start a family soon.

Now here we were almost ten years later. Lying in bed beside Ross, I brushed my hand softly against his cheek. He stirred slightly, his eyes trying to flutter open. "Good morning, honey," I said. He clasped my hand in his and pecked me on the cheek. Then he reached into the nightstand and brought out the devotional book that we read together every morning. Then we prayed, thanking God for His many blessings, asking for His continued watch care over us, and praying that we might serve Him according to His will.

With the little remaining time, we made quick plans for the day. "I have a faculty meeting at 9:00," I said, "so I can drop the kids off on my way. Lela Kathryn's class is going on a field trip today, so I have to take the chocolate cupcakes I made for them last night. She's so excited about going to that new technology museum and then to the park for a picnic. I'm glad it finally turned warm so she can wear the pink shorts set I bought her a few weeks ago." Lela Kathryn, seven years and four months old, looked cute in pink, with her dark brown hair and her beautiful brown eyes.

Ross smiled, knowing only too well his daughter's fondness for pretty clothes. "Well," he said, "I have classes all morning; then I have to meet with a student at 2:00. But I can pick Allen up from daycare after that, and he can go with me later to get Lela Kathryn from school. I'll have time to start dinner so we can eat early, before my night class. Do you want me to cook some spaghetti and green beans?"

"That'd be great," I said, thinking particularly about our youngest. Allen had just turned two and had recently acquired a taste for spaghetti. He had liked green beans ever since he was able to pick them up one at a time and put them in his mouth. We all liked chocolate, so I whispered my contribution to dinner. "I'll keep out some cupcakes for our dessert." Ross grinned, knowing that I wouldn't think a meal was complete without dessert.

Finally leaving our cozy bed, we got dressed and went in to get the children up. Lela Kathryn was already awake and had laid out her clothes – yes, just as I thought, the pink shorts set. Allen was harder to wake up; but when his Daddy said, "How about some pancakes for breakfast?" our little boy with the curly hair came alive.

I always liked mealtime at our house. Ross and I thought alike that this should be family time. The four of us took turns saying the blessing. Ross and I modeled a simple blessing like "We thank you, God, for this food. We pray that it will make us strong so we can be your helpers here on earth. Amen." When it was the children's turn, we gave them free reign to say whatever was on their minds. Lela Kathryn always prayed for the little children who were hungry. Allen, just beginning to talk in short sentences, might say something like "Tank-oo for cakes."

We often let the children help prepare the meals. Lela Kathryn liked to bake cookies – the kind you break apart and place on a cookie sheet. She even knew how to set the timer. Allen liked to stir – really hard – so we let him help make Jello with fruit in it. Whenever the children had a hand in preparing a dish, we made a big deal about how good it was.

And so went life – the life in my dreams.

Lessons Learned at Disney World

Walt Disney World may seem to be a somewhat unconventional place in which to learn spiritual truths, but when the eyes and ears of our hearts are watching and listening, we see and hear much more than physical sights and sounds. The spiritual truths that come to me every day affect the way I live.

My learning experience at Disney World began at the baggage claim area of Orlando International Airport. As I sat there, keeping watch over our luggage, I noticed a lady cradling a child as one does an infant. But this child wasn't a baby. He was perhaps eight or ten years old. My eyes riveted toward him, for I knew even at first glance that he must have cerebral palsy. His head wobbled uncontrollably – a sure sign that his body couldn't obey his mind's commands.

Nearby sat a small wheelchair, and soon a kindly man came and gently lifted the young boy into the chair. Accompanying the frail little body was an array of tubes which the man carefully adjusted, along with all the straps needed to secure the little boy's unsteady frame. Once situated in his chair, the child was surrounded by people who appeared to be more family members. Another young boy, most likely his brother, stroked his thick brown hair and spoke softly to him.

The scene looked like it had been played out thousands of times. The tenderness, the unconditional love, the care – these were not newly formed; indeed, they were seasoned, refined, and strengthened by each passing day. The young boy, unable to speak, responded in the only way he could – with squeals of pleasure at being loved. And as they rolled away, it was obvious that for this family that was enough. To give without counting the cost, to give everything and be content with what is given back, knowing that it too is everything – everything that one young boy has to give. And God, on that first Christmas, gave all of Himself to us. There is no equivalent repayment. But all He asks is our love.

Disney World is truly a magical place, as emphasized by the name of its first theme park, the Magic Kingdom. Inside the Magic Kingdom, our first ride was "It's a Small World." The animated figures all along the tiny canal dance, fly, and sing as they depict the many nationalities of the world – a world of hope and a world of fears, a world of laughter and a world of tears. There's so much to be shared that it's a small world after all! And isn't that the way God intended – that we share His Spirit and His love throughout the world!

The Spectro-Magic parade of lights was our treat for that evening. The long, frigid wait before the parade gave me a chance to get acquainted with my wheelchair neighbor. He had had a stroke three years before and still remained paralyzed in one leg. He was a compassionate man; and when he realized that my disability began at birth, he said quietly, "Life's not always fair." I pondered that statement; but then I saw the relationship between him and his wife and children, and I thought of my relationship with God and with my family and friends, and I reasoned that fairness comes in many forms, not the least of which is love.

On our day at MGM Studios, we saw a production of "The Lion King." The words of the Lion King to his son Simba struck a chord of familiarity with me. The great Lion King said to Simba, "Always remember who you are." Soon thereafter, the Lion King was killed, and Simba wandered for a long time through the forest with no thought that he should be exerting his powers of leadership. Simba had to be reminded that he was a child of the Lion King. I was reminded that we must live in constant awareness that we are children of the King of Kings.

The performance of "Beauty and the Beast" portrayed in musical gaiety the profound truth that in order to be human, one must learn to love another. Beauty loved the Beast even in his ghoulish state; and when he loved her in return, he became human again – a prince even. Are we not reminded of the Biblical statement concerning Jesus: "We love Him because He first loved us." (I John 4:19)

One of the most thrilling events was Epcot's candlelight processional featuring a 400-voice choir extolling the birth of the Savior. The Biblical account of Jesus' birth was read with power and conviction, each section followed by a perfectly chosen carol. The orchestra, the leader, and all 400 voices radiated an indescribable joy and thrill as they sang out in perfect harmony the wonder of Christmas...when, on the night Christ was born, "the soul felt its worth." As a final reminder to us all, the choir rang out, "Let there be peace on earth, and let it begin with me." With one heart, the entire audience stood in reverence and confirmation of the true spirit of Christmas.

Then there was the great laser and fireworks display called "Illuminations," preceded by the voice of Sandi Patty filling the air with "O Holy Night." How awesome to see thousands of people standing in silent acclaim of the Savior's birth!

The meaning of Jesus' sacrifice was affirmed to me that night in one of those ways that God has of talking to us through the most common events imaginable. As we left Epcot, I casually noticed that a good many people were turning in their wheelchairs at the gate. How I wanted to turn mine in and walk on!

But then God spoke from deep within my heart and reminded me that one day, at the gate of heaven, I will turn my wheelchair in and walk on with Him – all because of Christmas and all because of Calvary.